DEATH

ROW

DEATH ROW

ROW

THE FINAL MINUTES

MICHELLE LYONS

BLINK
bringing you closer

Published by Blink Publishing
2.25, The Plaza,
535 Kings Road,
Chelsea Harbour,
London, SW10 0SZ

www.blinkpublishing.co.uk

facebook.com/blinkpublishing
twitter.com/blinkpublishing

Hardback – 978-1-911-600-62-6
Trade paperback – 978-1-911-600-69-5
Paperback – 978-1-788-701-49-5
Ebook – 978-1-788-700-44-3

A CIP catalogue of this book is available from the British Library.

Typeset by seagulls.net
Printed and bound in Great Britain by Clays Ltd, Elcograf S.p.A.

3 5 7 9 10 8 6 4 2

Copyright © Michelle Lyons, 2018
Written with Ben Dirs
First published by Blink Publishing in 2018
First published as a paperback by Blink Publishing in 2018

Blink Publishing is an imprint of Bonnier Books UK
www.bonnierbooks.co.uk

CONTENTS

To my Mum, Dad and brother, for making me all that I am.

To my daughter, for making me realise all that I still want to be.

AUTHOR'S NOTE

While this is essentially the story of my time working with and for the Texas Department of Criminal Justice, first as a journalist and then as a spokesperson, it could not have been written without my dear friend and former colleague Larry Fitzgerald, whose thoughts appear throughout. As such, I must thank Ed Hancox, whose documentary about Larry for the BBC (*The Man Who Witnessed 219 Executions*) was the germ of this book and whose interviews, which he kindly shared with me, proved invaluable. In total, Larry and I witnessed almost 500 executions, many of them together. He was my mentor, a wonderful man, and will always be the face of the Texas prison system. This is Larry's story, as much as it is mine.

Michelle Lyons,
May 2018

PROLOGUE
A SINGLE TEAR

I can't remember his name, his crime or what Texas county he fell from, but the contours of his face are etched on my mind, as if he was executed yesterday. He was a black man, well into middle age, with a long, proud chin. But what I remember most is the nothingness. No family members, no friends, no comfort. Maybe he didn't want them to come, maybe they didn't care, maybe he didn't have any in the first place. There was nobody bearing witness for his victim, either. At least that's how I remember it. Maybe they were afraid, maybe they couldn't afford to make the trip, maybe he committed his crime so long ago that the authorities couldn't find anybody. Whatever the reason, it was just a prison official and two reporters, including me, looking through the glass at this man strapped fast to the gurney, needles in both arms, staring hard at the ceiling.

The man didn't look to the side. Why would he? There was nobody in the witness rooms he knew. But he would have been aware of the warden hovering by his head, and the chaplain, whose hand was rested just below his knee. When the warden stepped forward and asked if he wanted to make a last statement, the man barely shook his head, said nothing, and started blinking. That's when I saw it: a single tear at the corner of his right eye. A tear he desperately wanted to blink away, a tear he didn't want us to see. It pooled there for a moment, before running down his cheek. That tear affected me in ways no words could. The warden gave his signal, the chemicals started flowing, the man coughed, sputtered and exhaled. A doctor entered the room, pronounced the man dead and pulled a sheet over his head.

Because I can still see his face, I could probably go through my files and figure out who he was. But I don't want to remember his name, the crime he committed or where it happened. None of that matters. I remember his execution, and that's enough. As long as I live, I will never see anybody so lonely and forgotten.

While I was watching men and women die in the Texas death chamber – first as a reporter, then as part of the prison system – I didn't allow myself to travel down this road of introspection. When I look at my old execution notes, I can see that things bothered me. But because I was young and bold, everything was black and white and certain. Any misgivings I had, I shoved into a suitcase in my mind, which I kicked into a corner. If I had started exploring how the executions made me feel while I was seeing them, or gave too much thought to all the emotions that were in play, how would I have been able to go back into that room, month after month, year after year? What if I'd sobbed? What if someone had noticed the dread on my face? I just couldn't let my head go to that place. It was the numbness that preserved me and kept me going. But by the end, that suitcase was so full, I was squeezing misgivings in there and having to sit on it in a hurry.

It was only when I left the prison system, having witnessed at least 280 executions in 11 years, that I started thinking in detail about the things I'd seen. I'd suddenly see the big, brown plastic container of fruit punch, put out for the condemned man in the holding cell; or I'd open a bag of chips and smell the death chamber; or something on the radio would remind me of a conversation I'd had with an inmate, hours before he died. I'd picture the man on the gurney with the single tear, or the mother of child-killer Ricky McGinn. Despite being old and frail and confined to a wheelchair, Mrs McGinn turned up to her son's execution in her Sunday best, a floral dress and pearls. When the time came for McGinn to make his final statement, she struggled out of her chair and pressed her wrinkled hands against the glass, because she wanted to make absolutely sure he could see her before he slipped into the abyss.

When I was a little girl, I would lie in bed at night and cry, thinking about all the people I loved who were going to die. I can still picture the light green walls of my bedroom and hear the TV downstairs. I'd turn on my radio and hope the music might drown out my thoughts of death. I'd look through the open doorway, onto the light in the hallway, tears streaming down my cheeks. But I never thought to go downstairs and tell my mom and dad my fears, it was always my secret to deal with. What made me feel better was the thought that when we died, we'd all end up in heaven together. Why be afraid of loved ones dying if death wasn't really a loss? We'd all meet again, it was just a matter of when.

As I grew older, my fear of death developed into a fear of being forgotten. I blame my first love in high school. We broke up when I moved with my family from Texas to Illinois, and within weeks he was seeing someone else. I was devastated. Apparently, I wasn't as important as I thought I was. I couldn't understand how somebody could love me so much but forget me so quickly. It sounds dumb, but it messed me up for years. Every time a relationship ended, I thought: 'Did I pack a punch? Will they remember me?' That's why when I die, I want to be cremated and tossed somewhere pretty. There's nothing sadder than a little stone somewhere that nobody ever visits. Lonely and forgotten, like the man whose name and crime I can't remember.

CHAPTER 1
GOING TO SLEEP

'If a man were torn to pieces in my presence it would not
have been so repulsive as this ingenious and elegant machine
by means of which they killed a strong, hale, healthy man
in an instant.'

Leo Tolstoy, on the execution of Francis Richeux, 6 April 1857

'This was my first execution and I was completely fine with it.
Many, many people asked me if I was really okay. I really was.
In fact, I felt bad, like, "Am I supposed to be upset about this?
Do people think I'm evil or something because I'm not?"'

Michelle's journal, on the execution of Javier Cruz, 1 October 1998

An inmate once told me I brought sunshine to death row. He's not the only one. Do you know how many people have told me I radiate light? On a recent trip to London, a colleague told me that she enjoys doing things with me, because I have a 'genuine enthusiasm'. A lot of people have told me similar things: that my enthusiasm is child-like, that I'm youthful, that I always seem happy. Some of this is true. I genuinely get excited about crushed ice, hand fans, cheese fries, light-up toys, novelty cups and pretty much anything covered in glitter or rhinestones. I get weirdly competitive at board games and never just *let* children win. I love scavenger hunts and mystery games and escape rooms. I let people believe that is all I am, because I hate letting anyone down, no matter how life, or the people in it, let me down. I will gather friends around a table, drink cocktails and entertain them with sarcastic quips and stories, because that is what people have come to expect of me. I joke around, because it makes me uncomfortable to talk about serious things. I am comically self-deprecating, especially about things that have brought me pain. But, in secret, I cry more than any of them would think. I have a pocket of inner darkness that sometimes consumes me and makes me want to shut out the world. That's how I feel now, thinking about the things I saw and heard in that death chamber. I can't get the tears to stop rolling down my cheeks.

It's a big deal to be born in Galveston. In Texas, people ask all the time: 'Oh, are you a BOI?' Meaning, was I 'born on the island'. I even have a BOI sticker on my car. My brother was born off the island and I like to tell him that he's inferior to me for that very reason.

Galveston was a cool place to grow up, very laid-back in a lot of ways. I had a summer job in one of the tacky souvenir shops and friends who worked as lifeguards or on burger stands. We had a condo right on Seawall Boulevard, with a view of the beach, and a hunting cabin up in Texas Hill Country, which my dad, uncles and grandpa built themselves from scratch. There was no electricity, a wood-burning stove for heat and a giant rain-water tank. It was rugged and remote and there were scorpions, snakes and all sorts of freaky bugs. All we had for entertainment was this big radio that stayed on around the clock, playing old country songs. I felt so safe and content, curled up in bed in the dark, listening to the grown-ups talk and laugh and play cards with the radio playing softly in the background.

My father started his career as a journalist in Galveston, which is how he met my mom – he was a dashing young police reporter and she was this young, foxy thing working as a records clerk at the

Galveston Police Department. I remember hugging him when he got home from working at the *Galveston County Daily News*, and inhaling the comforting smell of newspaper ink. It's still one of my favourite scents. When I was 16, we moved to Illinois, where my dad got a job as a publisher of *The Benton Evening News*. Benton is a quiet little town, with a population of less than 10,000, but it's had its brush with infamy: shortly before we moved there, four members of the Dardeen family were viciously murdered in the town. The father was found dead in a field with his genitals stuffed in his mouth, and the mother and son were found beaten to death in their trailer. Even worse, while being beaten, the mother gave birth, and the baby was battered to death as well. Bizarrely, one of the prime suspects – a guy named Tommy Sells, who they believe killed 20-odd people in total – wound up years later on Texas death row, and I ended up face to face with him in the interview room.

Moving to Benton meant breaking up with my boyfriend and losing my first love, but I soon found a new one: the *Evening News* needed a darkroom technician, so that became my job, even though I was still in high school. I would go to work at 6 a.m. every day, the photographers would bring me their film and I'd develop it. My hands were a mess, because of the chemicals, and I ruined most of my clothes, but I delighted in that job. I became a photographer, a 17-year-old covering car wrecks and fires. I had no issues taking those kinds of pictures, except for one time I was dispatched to a wreck involving a girl I went to school with, I got upset and refused to get close. My dad said, 'You need to get in there!' And I finally snapped: 'I can't! I know her!' I shoved the camera into his chest and walked away. Later, he impressed upon me that, as a journalist, there would be times I'd witness scenes that would disturb me, but I'd have to do it anyway, in order to relay the news to the public, which was what I was being paid to do. I came to realise he was right. It taught me that I was doing a job, and if you're doing a job, you need to do your best, even if it means having to take pictures of someone you know who might be badly injured.

Although my parents wanted me to go into journalism, I was a rebellious teenager and decided to study business at Texas A&M University instead. I didn't know what type of business I wanted to go into, but I pictured myself wearing cute suits and making lots of money. But after a few business math classes, I realised I was awful at it. So I took a journalism class, just to see if I might like it, which I did. I switched my major to journalism, and a wonderful professor named Ed Walraven set me up with a job at the local newspaper, *The Bryan-College Station Eagle*. There was no going back from there.

I thought I was going to be reviewing restaurants, but was the obituary girl instead. I'd get all these forms from local funeral homes and write up these dead people's lives, some of them fascinating, most of them humdrum. I had a stint as the police reporter, during which I covered a Christmas Day escape from a county jail and an explosion in an oil field in a little town called Dime Box. One of the workers was killed by the explosion while he was standing on a platform, and he'd died where he was leaning. Because of the flames, they couldn't get close enough to remove his body, so I watched it burn all day, until it was a charred, black figure. It was disturbing, but somebody had to cover this stuff. Even though I was a young college student, I was also a police reporter, and I wanted to be good at it, so I never let things get to me.

Looking back, it seems inevitable that I'd end up working in death, and it's true that I've always had a macabre side and a wicked sense of humour. I've always been interested in crime, and Texas is a hotbed of the craziest crime stories. I also like mysteries, riddles, puzzles, anything that needs to be solved. It's probably why I'm interested in smart, complex, multi-dimensional people. What makes them tick? Why do they think in a certain way? What makes them do what they do? And in the prison system, there's a whole population of people whose brains work differently than the norm.

After stints at the *Chicago Sun-Times* and a newspaper in Leavenworth, Kansas, my dad took a job as the publisher of *The Huntsville Item*, about 70 miles north of Houston and 45 minutes from College Station, where I was still a student. I met the editor of the *Item* at a job fair in 1998, found out they had an opening, interviewed for the job and got it. My dad had no idea. The managing editor went into his office one day and said, 'Hey, good news, we've filled that reporting position.' My dad said, 'Great. Who is it?', and the managing editor told him it was me. Later, my dad said he was a bit unsure about it, because either people might think I was the favoured one or he would have to be harder on me. It was the latter route he went down.

My first beat was city government, with a hodgepodge of things thrown in, like covering the local hospital and writing feature stories. Because it was a small newspaper with only three reporters, it was not uncommon for me to write three to five stories a day. Suddenly, I was a big fish in a little pond, and I loved it. One day, the woman who covered the Texas Department of Criminal Justice (TDCJ) wasn't able to witness an execution, so I was asked to step in – not only are a victim's and inmate's loved ones invited to witness in the death chamber, but there are also spots for five reporters, with one always set aside for the *Item*. My dad called me to his office and asked, 'Can you handle it?' And I said, 'Yeah, I've got this. This is not going to be a problem for me.'

The woman I replaced gave me a rundown of what was going to happen that night: I'd go to an office building across from the Walls Unit, where all the executions in Texas take place, and meet a guy named Larry Fitzgerald, who was the manager of the TDCJ Public Information Office; he'd take me to his office, where we'd hang out until we got the call. Then, I'd be escorted to a witness room in the death chamber, where the inmate would already be laid out on a gurney, with the IV lines attached to his arms. He'd make a last statement, he'd go to sleep, and I'd return to the office to write my story. That's how it was presented to me and that's exactly what happened.

Javier Cruz had killed two elderly men in San Antonio in 1991, so I went into the death chamber thinking, 'Hmmm, this man beat two old men to death with a hammer and he's just going to sleep? I can deal with that...' It really didn't bother me at all, to the extent that I don't remember much about Cruz's execution. I got back to the office, my dad asked if I was okay, and I said, 'I'm fine, I'm going to write the story.' I wrote it in less than an hour. I was 22.

'Looking to his family while repeating, "I'm okay," and waving aside his chance to make a last statement, 41-year-old Javier Cruz was put to death Thursday night – the 15th person to be executed this year in Texas...'

From Michelle's story on Javier Cruz, *The Huntsville Item*, 2 October 1998

CHAPTER 2
JUST A JOB

'The death penalty is unfair, arbitrary, capricious and fraught with racial discrimination and judicial bias.'

Bianca Jagger, anti-death penalty campaigner

'One thing he kept saying to me was, "I've killed three people and I'm going to kill you..."'

Lisa Blackburn, Gary Graham's final victim

After Kate Winslet filmed *The Life of David Gale* in Huntsville in 2001, she gave an interview in which she called the city 'one giant prison' and talked about its 'pervasive sense of death'. That was deeply dishonest. To be more blunt, it was ridiculous bullshit. I very much doubt she spent much time in Huntsville. I don't recall seeing her in line at Whataburger, and the filmmakers certainly didn't do much research. We only saw Kate once, when she was filming the final scene. In it, she runs what in real life would have been about 30 miles from death row to the Walls Unit, throws herself on the ground and starts yelling and screaming for them to stop the execution. I was standing there, shaking my head in disbelief. At one point, Kate got upset that there were too many of us watching and everybody had to scatter. I think we were cramping her art.

I took the criticism personally, because the city had been good to me. Huntsville, population 38,548 at the last count, is situated between Houston and Dallas, which is one of its main selling points. But it is a beautiful city in its own right, set among rolling hills and the trees that make up East Texas's so-called Piney Woods.

Huntsville is so picturesque that if you stopped off without knowing that it was home to seven prison units, and had been dubbed 'the execution capital of the world' by the European media, you could spend a pleasant day there and leave none the wiser. There is no heavy, negative energy in Huntsville, clinging to the place like a black fog, it's just a typical American city, with fairy lights decorating its downtown square at Christmas, American flags lining the streets during patriotic holidays and churches everywhere. When I moved to Huntsville, it was my intention to stay six months before moving to a bigger city. But that six months turned into a year, which turned into five, which turned into 10. Now it's been 20 years and I'm quite content.

The Walls Unit – more properly called the Huntsville Unit – was opened in 1849, making it the oldest state prison in Texas. Before 1924, hanging was the preferred method of execution in the state, and individual counties were responsible for carrying them out. But since 1924, every execution in Texas has taken place in the Walls Unit's death chamber. Between 1924 and 1964, 361 offenders were executed by 'Old Sparky', otherwise known as the electric chair. Charles Reynolds of Red River County was the first to go that way, and Joseph Johnson of Harris County the last. In 1972, the Supreme Court declared the death penalty to be unconstitutional, on the grounds that it was a cruel and unusual punishment. But Texas reinstated it less than two years later and adopted lethal injection as its new means of execution in 1977. In

1982, Charlie Brooks was the first offender to be executed by this new, less dramatic method.

Because the Walls Unit was built so long ago, the town grew up around it, and the prison system is the biggest employer in the city. The second would be the university, and even that has a significant focus on criminal justice – people come from all over the world to study corrections at Sam Houston State. They say that during the Great Depression, Huntsville was the only community in Texas that wasn't affected, because they were still locking up a whole bunch of people, perhaps even more than usual, because poverty breeds crime.

If you don't work for the prison system, it's likely somebody in your family does. Around Huntsville, you bump into people all the time who work for TDCJ, or whose husband or wife or brother or sister work for TDCJ. You see officers all over town, wearing their distinctive uniforms – all-grey, or grey pants and a blue shirt with a state seal on it. Stores offer discounts to prison employees and even cater to inmates who have just been released. When an inmate gets out on parole, they're given street clothes, and they're usually pretty crappy. But they're also given a $50 cheque, so businesses will offer to cash that cheque and stores will sell cheap T-shirts, tank tops and bandanas, pretty much anything that inmate needs.

Even though Huntsville isn't far from College Station, where I went to college, and I was aware that Huntsville was where executions took place, I'd never given the death penalty much thought before seeing Javier Cruz die on the gurney. In fact, I didn't give the death penalty much thought after seeing Javier Cruz die on the gurney. I was pro-death penalty, and thought it was the most appropriate punishment for certain crimes, such as rape and murder and killing children. If you rape and kill a child, there's something fundamentally wrong with you, you can't redeem yourself. Yet despite Texas having the death penalty, there's not a lot of discussion about it. Like a lot of social issues, people tend not to engage with it unless it directly affects them. For most Texans, the death penalty is an abstract concept, occasionally debated at dinner parties.

But it became far more real for me when I took over the prison beat for *The Huntsville Item* in January 2000. George W. Bush had become Governor of Texas in 1995, and after a slow start – three people were executed in the state in 1996 – the death house sprang to life again. In 1997, 37 inmates were put to death, followed by 20 in 1998 and 35 in 1999. But I couldn't have predicted what would happen next. In my first month on the prison beat, I witnessed five men die. In 2000, 40 men and women were executed in the Huntsville death house, a record for the most executions in a single year by an individual state, and almost as many as the rest of the United States combined.

The first execution I witnessed in my new role was that of Earl Carl Heiselbetz Jr, who murdered a mother and her two-year-old daughter in Sabine County in 1991. His last words were, 'Love y'all, see you on the other side.' But when I look up those early executions in my journal, it's the mundane details that jump out at me. Heiselbetz was 'still wearing his glasses'; Betty Lou Beets, who murdered two of her five husbands and shot another in the back (and was only the second woman to be executed in Texas since the Civil War) had 'tiny little feet'; Jeffrey Dillingham, a hitman who had slashed the throat of a woman in Fort Worth, 'had these dimples and actually was a very good-looking man'.

Quite a few of the inmates reminded me of other people. Spencer Goodman, who murdered the wife of ZZ Top manager Bill Ham, 'looked like a friend of mine, Jeremy Johnson – they had the same build and there was something similar about their ankles and feet'; Odell Barnes Jr, who was executed for a 1989 rape and murder in Wichita Falls, 'looked like the star of the sitcom *Hangin' with Mr Cooper*'; Orien Joiner, who murdered two Lubbock waitresses in 1986, 'reminded me a whole lot of the Penguin from the movie *Batman*'; Thomas Mason, who murdered his estranged wife's mother and grandmother in Whitehouse in 1991, 'looked JUST like my grandfather... he kept doing this blinking and twitching that my grandpa does'. Also like Mason, my grandpa was from Tennessee and a tough old gun-toting guy who was always threatening to shoot someone. One difference: Grandpa never did.

A psychologist would probably have something to say about all these lookalikes I saw strapped to the gurney in the Texas death house – maybe that I was subconsciously trying to humanise these people who had done terrible things in order to soften the impact their execution might have on me, but I honestly think I was just being a blasé kid. It didn't bother me that Thomas Mason looked like my grandpa – I wasn't crying about it, because it wasn't actually my grandpa.

When I started living alone, before I started witnessing executions, I was afraid of coming home and finding someone hiding in my closet, to the extent that I used to get really freaked out about it. People would say, 'that stuff doesn't really happen'. But one of the first executions I witnessed, that's exactly what the guy did. James Clayton broke into a stranger's apartment, hid in the woman's closet and when she got home he killed her, apparently because his girlfriend had threatened to break up with him. But straight after seeing Clayton die, I went off, wrote my story and hit the bar.

Another time, the inmate's family turned on us reporters in the witness room, telling us we were part of 'this killing machine'. But that didn't bother me either, because that's not how I saw it. I was just a reporter, writing down what I was seeing. I didn't think I was part of anything. Being young was a huge advantage in that job. I was only 24 when I took over the prison beat, and that meant I was much better at removing myself from situations and compartmentalising the things I'd seen.

Friends would joke with me about my job, send me inappropriate emails and texts. But on the other hand, Houston cops covering homicides – people shot up and stabbed and dismembered – would tell me they wouldn't be able to watch an execution if you paid them. My brother, who saw far worse during his two tours of Iraq, didn't understand how I could walk into that death chamber and watch men die, again and again. But – and I don't mean this to sound flippant – I never would have been able to cut hair for a living. If I see a stray hair when I'm eating, I want to gag. One of my best friends was a hairdresser, and I'd say to her, 'How can you do what you do?' I guess everybody has their own poison, and maybe everybody is uniquely programmed to do the job they do.

Once they got to know me, and realised I had the stomach for it, correctional officers would show me pictures of inmates who'd killed themselves, including one death row inmate who had slit his own throat, so that his head was almost hanging off. And it didn't bother me. When you're a journalist, or at least a good journalist, you're built to be able to detach from proceedings, be dispassionate and discerning. Witnessing executions was just part of my job, and once I clocked off, I was able to forget about it.

But there are clues throughout my journal that I wasn't coping quite as well as I thought I was. In fact, I sound almost paranoid at times. After a handful of executions, I start fretting about the smell of the death chamber. I can smell it in my dad's office, when I open a bag of Cheetos and, after one execution, I start worrying that the smell has somehow seeped into my chewing gum. I thought it might be the actual chemicals I could smell, the three they used to execute the inmates. It couldn't have been, because the chemicals were sealed in syringes. But after one execution, I sound almost panicky: 'I wonder if MY lungs could collapse just from smelling the chemicals?' I hated that smell. I've never smelled anything else like it and I never want to smell it again. That's why I liked it when someone smuggled in a cigarette for an inmate's last meal, because you'd smell the lingering smoke instead.

It's a good thing I kept that journal, otherwise I'd be sitting here now, telling everybody that witnessing executions as a young reporter never moved me in the slightest. My journal contains evidence of empathy, whose existence I denied for so long. Billy Hughes was the first inmate I interviewed on death row, and the first inmate I'd interviewed that I later saw executed. He was very articulate and smart, very, very likeable and accomplished a lot of things during his 24 years in prison (which was, at the time, the second-longest stay in Texas death row history). He earned two college degrees, translated books into braille, ran a greeting card business, published a travel guide for horse riders, created a cartoon strip and worked from his cell as a registered anti-death penalty lobbyist.

Before his execution, his spiritual advisor told me that Hughes had liked the article I'd written about him, and, at least according to my journal, my eyes started burning. I guess I felt weirdly proud that my article had been one of the last things he'd read. But after the execution, the victim's mother called Hughes 'manipulative', and I wondered if I'd been manipulated, too. Later, Larry told me that Hughes thought he didn't deserve for me to be so nice about him, which made my heart sink. Although there was a theory that

Hughes took the hit for his wife, he was convicted of and executed for killing a state trooper, and it was my responsibility not to simply write down everything an inmate told me.

There was also William Kitchens, who was executed for the 1986 rape and murder of Patricia Webb in Abilene. According to my journal, I welled up during his last statement, apparently because his apology seemed so sincere. And there was Oliver Cruz, who was the second of two inmates to be executed on the same night – what they call a 'double-header' in the prison trade. The first, Brian Roberson, who had stabbed his two elderly neighbours to death, was an asshole. Just before the drugs kicked in, he turned to his victims' families and said, 'Be careful when y'all are driving home – don't have no wreck and kill yourselves...' They were his last words on earth. Twenty minutes later, we were back in the death chamber and Cruz was tearful and apologising to his victim's family. He looked so small and young and had this thin moustache, like Hispanic teenagers have when they're trying to look like a man. His victim, a US Air Force officer named Kelly Donovan, had been out walking when she was abducted by Cruz and an accomplice. After raping Donovan, Cruz stabbed her to death. A priest, Father Emmanuel McCarthy, who was in town for the execution, told a reporter that because Donovan was wearing short shorts, 'nothing good was going to come of that'. In other words, the man of God thought she was asking for it.

Having turned himself in, Cruz admitted to killing three other people. But watching him plead for forgiveness on the gurney, I felt sorry for him. In fact, according to my diary, 'I felt sorry for him in a way that is difficult to put into words.' I just appreciated it when a condemned man admitted his guilt, rather than lying to the bitter end.

There are other entries in my journal that make me cringe, because I sound stupid, immature and smug. As someone who has always felt very strongly about owning their behaviour, some of the things I read from that period make me extremely uncomfortable. After the execution of Stacey Lamont, on 14 November 2000, I wrote, 'Here's the deal: if you're going to do this job, you better be at least a little tough. I'm not a mean or cold person. I cried when I saw *Titanic* and when my hamster died. It's just that this is my job. Pansy-asses. That's all I have to say.'

I had no right to be so self-righteous, because I knew almost nothing about life and death. I was an adult, but I was still a kid in so many ways, and because I was still a kid, everything was cut and dried. I remember Mike Graczyk of the Associated Press, who had witnessed hundreds of executions, being asked by a TV crew how he felt, having just witnessed yet another one. Graczyk stopped typing, looked at them and said, 'My only thoughts are about getting this story out.' That impressed me. Reporters were supposed to be dispassionate, detached from the action, because we were just doing a job.

After one execution, a female reporter ran to the bathroom crying, and I remember listening to her and her friend and thinking, 'I'm going to freak out on these people...' There was a female journalist from England who started crying because the inmate looked like her boyfriend. I just thought those chicks were weak. As a journalist, you've just got to suck things up. But I could be callous and insufferable in those days – 'oh, I'm so much tougher than you...'

At other times in my journal, I sound like a moody teenager. For whatever reason, Paul Nuncio gets it both barrels: 'This little man got on my nerves so very badly. First of all, he couldn't make sense to save his life. Secondly, he was so disrespectful to the victim's relatives. Thirdly, he just had a stupid look on his face.' To be fair, Nuncio did rape and strangle a woman to death, and I suspect anybody would cringe at some of the things they wrote in their journal when they were 24. That said, my entry on Tommy Ray Jackson makes for almost unbearable reading. Jackson, who was executed for the 1983 kidnapping, rape and murder of University of Texas student Rosalind Robinson, delivered a rambling last statement which went on for nine minutes, way longer than normal. The whole time he was talking, I was getting more and more irritated, because I wanted to get my story written and hit the bars for the Mexican celebration of Cinco de Mayo. So this guy is lying on a gurney, trying to prolong his life for a few precious extra minutes, while I'm getting annoyed that he's eating into happy hour. What a dick. That's ugly and makes me feel embarrassed and ashamed.

In my defence, it's no surprise I was already showing signs of fraying, even if I didn't acknowledge it at the time: in the first six months of 2000, I witnessed 22 inmates die, including seven in May alone. And a few of those executions qualified as bona fide circuses.

On the day of his execution, Billy Hughes said to Larry Fitzgerald, 'I'm really sorry for everything that's gonna be happening out there', but didn't go into any more detail. When I arrived at the Walls Unit, there were tons of uniformed state troopers on one lawn, which would always happen when a law enforcement officer was murdered. But at the other end of the street, there was a scoreboard which read, 'George 117–2 Jeb', a reference to the number of executions that had taken place under the governorships of George W. Bush in Texas and his brother Jeb in Florida. There was also a marching band and some cheerleaders, in letter-sweaters and pleated skirts, chanting stuff like, 'Texas is good, Texas is great, we kill more than any other state!'

The whole thing had been set up by documentary maker Michael Moore, for his TV show *The Awful Truth*. Almost any other execution, fine. But when you've got a whole bunch of state troopers standing stoically, all in uniform in honour of their fallen colleague, that's kind of awful. It was Hughes who almost made me laugh out loud during his last statement, when he said, 'If I'm paying my debt to society, I am due a rebate and a refund.' I snickered and then thought, 'Oh my God, I'm not supposed to do that. Not here, not now...'

Ponchai Wilkerson, the son of a retired sheriff's deputy, shot dead a jewellery shop clerk in Houston in 1990. The murder of

Chung Myong Yi was the culmination of a month-long crime spree, which included drive-by shootings, robberies and car thefts. Wilkerson was also one of the liveliest inmates Texas death row had ever hosted. On Thanksgiving night 1998, he attempted to escape from death row with six other condemned prisoners. Wilkerson and five others surrendered when officers started shooting at them, but Martin Gurule kept going. What did he have to lose? A week later, Gurule – who was the first person to break out of Texas death row since the Bonnie and Clyde era – was found dead in the Trinity River, presumably having drowned. He had magazines and cardboard under his clothes, which acted as a suit of armour, enabling him to roll over two razor-wire security fences.

My introduction to Wilkerson came in February 2000, when he and another inmate, Howard Guidry, took a female guard hostage at the Terrell Unit (later renamed the Polunsky Unit) in Livingston, where Texas death row had recently been moved after Gurule's breakout. Wilkerson had somehow opened his cell door, overpowered the guard and shackled her in a day room. He and Guidry were armed with sharpened pieces of metal. When I found out what was going on, I hopped in my car and eventually found the unit at the end of a dark, remote road. I arrived to discover that it had been shut down and there were journalists all along the street and ditch outside, because they couldn't get near the parking lot. Suddenly, Larry Fitzgerald came striding down the road in his hand-tooled cowboy boots, and I remember thinking, 'This guy is such a badass.' I'd met him before at a couple of executions, but hadn't really gotten to know him. But now, amid all that chaos, he was the coolest, calmest person there, and exuded charisma. To a kid who was new in the job, he was very impressive. He gave the media a briefing and set up a plan, which is exactly the way you should do it: if you're not transparent with journalists, they'll make shit up.

Larry Fitzgerald

My background was broadcasting. I was a disc jockey for a while – me and my wife Marianne didn't have much money, but we had all the records we could eat. I worked for radio stations all over Texas – Taylor, Bryan, Dallas – before becoming a news reporter. There was just so much going on back then: the assassination of JFK, Vietnam, Black Power, hippies, women's lib, Watergate and the resignation of Nixon. I loved that world dearly.

When I was working for KXOL in Fort Worth, they had this big peace march at the University of Texas, and they were covering our mobile news unit with flowers and handing out marijuana to everybody. When I got home, Marianne said to me, 'Did you smoke some and go on air?' And I said, 'No, not me...' Me and Marianne met in 1959, at a beer joint in Austin called Dirty Martin's. That was back in the days of car hops, and if you knew a crazy guy called Doc, he'd sell you beer if you were underage. After we were married, we lived in a scary-looking two-storey apartment in Taylor, Texas. I took Marianne to see Psycho, *when she was pregnant. She was terrified, so when we got home,*

I switched all the lights off and stood at the top of the stairs, making the slashing sound from the famous shower scene. She saw the funny side, eventually.

I shared a jail cell with Jane Fonda in Fort Hood. She was protesting about the soldiers leaving for Vietnam, I kept sticking my microphone in her face, and we both wound up getting arrested. She did not shut up the whole time we were in that cell together. When I joined the prison system, it turned out one of the wardens was the cop who arrested me that day. I got into trouble sometimes with the bosses, and quit one radio job because the owner was an asshole. One Austin station I worked at was owned by future president Lyndon B. Johnson, who was a senator at the time. I recall he'd come around turning off the lights, to save on electricity.

It wasn't always good being my wife. We had two small kids, I never changed a diaper in my life, and Marianne never knew what was going to happen next. Somebody had to keep putting bread on the table, and she must have worried that I was never going to settle down. But I had an optimistic outlook on life, always thought something would come up, and it always did.

When I moved up to be a news director in Fort Worth, I really got to know the movers and shakers in the community, the people who were creating the news – the lawyers, the judges, the politicians. I liked being on the inside, seeing things most people didn't, having a preview of what was going to happen. More than anything else, I liked being able to ask difficult questions. It was that curiosity that made me a good journalist. I wanted to tell people what was going on, and I was good at telling stories and painting pictures on the radio. That was my talent. If there was a catastrophe – a car wreck or a train crash – I'd be there. There's a certain adrenalin flow that comes with that sort of stuff.

In those days, there were no cell phones or computers, so you had to go in person to the cop shop to get stories. I had a car fitted with police radio, and one time, when I was driving home from work, I got wind that a shooting was taking place in a bar in Mansfield. I pulled up in the parking lot at about the same time as the sheriff's deputy, and there was still gunfire going on inside. When we finally made it in there, there were dead people all over the floor, and it turned out a gentleman had walked into this bar and started shooting people at random. He ran into a restroom and some of the survivors followed him in with knives and killed him as he was trying to reload his .45. Yeah, that was pretty exciting.

When I was working for KCLE in Cleburne, there was an underground explosion near the town. It turned out it was the site of a top-secret factory, making bombs to drop on Vietnam. There was also the time some prisoners escaped and were hiding out in the hills of West Texas. Everyone with a rifle was out there hunting for them, but all I had was a notebook. When I was working for KXOL, in the city of Hurst, we stumbled upon a shootout at an illegal gambling den, on Fort Worth's east side. We were there before the cops, and were lucky not to get shot. But I just wanted to be where the action was, no matter what was going down. I also covered the case of Thomas Cullen Davis, the Texas oil heir who stood trial for the murder of his stepdaughter. I had to shave my beard off, because people kept confusing me with the boyfriend of Davis's wife. Davis was acquitted, before standing trial again for conspiring to murder his wife and the judge overseeing their divorce proceedings. Guess what? Davis got off again. In Texas, it's often said, 'If you don't have the capital, you get the punishment', and the opposite is true. It wasn't all bad news, like the time an 18-wheeler turned over on a freeway and hundreds of chickens escaped. Every person in the vicinity who owned a gunny sack was out on that freeway catching dinner.

After falling out with one of the station owners, I had a spell as a truck driver, working for a guy named Bo Powell, who owned a company called Anything Anywhere After Midnight. I did a lot of strange hauls, I can tell you, until one of the trucks, which was carrying oil, caught fire in Tyler. After that, I decided driving trucks wasn't really for me. In 1978, I joined the State Bar of Texas, as director of communications. I think Marianne was relieved, because she knew I was going to get a pay cheque every month.

I had a way of getting things out of people, so I heard a lot of important people spill their guts. But it was an overwhelming job, and that's when I really started drinking. Why do you think they call it a bar? If I walked into pretty much anywhere and saw a media type I knew, I'd pick up the tab. I'd have a $3,000 American Express bill every month, and it did my liver no favours at all. You find out a lot of things in bars, and drinking relaxed me, was a crutch, made it that I didn't have to think about the pressures of the job. But it also meant I wound up in Alcoholics Anonymous.

After leaving the Bar of Texas in 1991, I went to work for the Texas Department of Commerce as a location scout. Me and the cameraman Jim would drive all night long to destinations the length and breadth of Texas, covering shrimp fests in Port Aransas and catfish fests in Conroe. I did media for Bill Hobby's run for lieutenant governor and Ann Richards' second campaign for the governorship of Texas. When the David Koresh thing was going down in Waco, and the Branch Davidian cult went up in flames, Richards was releasing a falcon in Big Bend Park. A reporter asked her about Koresh and she didn't know anything about it. I got it both barrels, and she didn't get re-elected.

A guy named Larry Todd managed the public information office at the Texas Department of Criminal Justice and was an old friend of mine from our days in Dallas-Fort Worth radio, and when he asked me to apply for a job as a spokesman, I jumped at the chance. I didn't really ask any questions, because I was out of work and needed money. That's the only reason I applied. At my interview, I was asked how I felt about executions, and replied, 'I'm ambivalent.' It was only later I discovered that it was part of my job description to witness so many of those damn things. I honestly thought I was being hired as a technician, to work with the Texas legislature on prison matters. Marianne thought the idea of me witnessing executions was terrible.

I also assumed that the job would be based in Austin, which is where I lived, so when they told me I'd be working out of Huntsville,

I thought, 'Huntsville? That's the sticks, man, I don't wanna live in Huntsville!' I came out of Austin, which is a pretty liberal town, and I'd always vowed that I'd never end up living east of Interstate 35. I had no idea what to expect living in East Texas. But I didn't have a choice, I was just an old media man who needed a job.

I started work for TDCJ in January 1995, and was soon asking myself the question, 'How in the hell did a guy like me ever get hired by TDCJ?' Huntsville is a pretty town, full of friendly people. But it's a conservative community, behind East Texas's Pine Curtain, on the buckle of the Bible Belt. The Baptists and the Pentecostals have a big presence, and it's not unusual to see people praying over their meals in a restaurant. If Huntsville is conservative, TDCJ is on another level entirely, to the extent that I was a little bit taken aback by it. I wouldn't describe myself as a liberal, but I would have been identified as a Democrat. I guess being a Democrat in Huntsville is the same as being a liberal.

Because I came from Austin, the administration also thought I was a politician, which is the worst thing you can be in the prison system. Those early days were tough. There were a lot of phone calls that didn't get returned and it was a nomadic life, living in a motel in Huntsville and driving back to Austin every weekend. But after a couple of months, I was given state housing, which meant going back to Austin every two weeks. I started getting invited to barbeques and drinks and meetings with the people in charge, and eventually, after about a year, I was accepted. I could see people thinking, 'Well, he's actually an okay guy.'

I knew nothing about prisons when I started, and had never spent much time around convicts. I thought they just locked 'em up and threw away the key. I also hadn't really given the death penalty much thought. I was a total neophyte. But TDCJ wanted a grey beard, somebody who had been around the block a few times, which I had. They also needed someone who could deal with media pressure, although I had no idea how great that pressure would be. But I had been armed with one piece of advice that served me well. A friend of mine, who I'd worked with at the State Bar of Texas, told me, 'Larry, if you go down there and treat the offenders with respect, you will have the best job in the world. But if you go down there and are an asshole, you'll hate it.' So I decided I was going to treat those people with respect...

Wilkerson and Guidry eventually surrendered, and less than a month later, the former was scheduled to be executed. But that hostage situation at Terrell wasn't Wilkerson's last stand. When he refused to leave his cell on death row, he was eventually gassed out, and he had to be carried to and from the van that taxied him to Huntsville. A five-man extraction team then dragged him from the holding cell to the death chamber, before they pinned him to the gurney using extra Velcro strapping and a bandage across his head. I was stationed in the victim's witness room, with Larry and Mike Graczyk, when Wilkerson gave his last statement, the chemicals started flowing and everything seemed to be going as planned. Suddenly, Wilkerson started twisting his tongue around in a weird circular motion. I saw something metal and thought he was trying to spit out his retainer. Then I realised he was saying something and I saw this little key pop out of his mouth, at the exact moment he died. The stand-in warden, Neill Hodges, stepped forward, snatched the key off Wilkerson's chin and stuck it in his pocket. We were all just standing there in shock. Eventually, I scribbled 'KEY?' on my notepad, showed it to Larry and he nodded. Holy shit.

> *'For a few seconds, I had the crazy thought, "He's going to get off that table and kill us." It was a kind of* Silence of the Lambs *moment, the part where Hannibal Lecter spat the paper clip out and you knew the guards were in trouble.'*
>
> **Michelle's journal, 14 March 2000**

Afterwards, all us reporters were scrambling around, trying to find out where the hell this key came from. We asked the chaplain, Jim Brazzil, what he said just before the key popped out of his mouth, and Brazzil said, 'The secret as of Wilkerson.' Apparently, Wilkerson had been jacking with the officers all day, telling them he knew something they didn't. Their response was, 'Whatever, Ponchai...' Presumably, his secret was that he had this handcuff key.

Later on, when they did the incident report, what they determined probably happened was that he'd planned to escape from his handcuffs on the way to Huntsville and either hijack the van or jump out of the door. What he didn't count on was that death row inmates have more than one set of handcuffs on them when they are being transported for their executions. So even if he had been able to remove one set, he wouldn't have been able to remove the other set. But it triggered a huge investigation, they did a big toss of the unit, and came up with more keys. It was Wilkerson's one last victory, him saying a big 'fuck you' to the system, which was what he seemed to have been put on earth to do. A few years later, when Hodges became the warden full-time, he had that key in a little frame in his office.

Betty Lou Beets also attracted a lot of media attention, simply because she was a woman. But the main event of 2000, by far, was the execution of Gary Graham, or Shaka Sankofa, as he preferred to be called.

I never understood why certain inmates ended up being cause célèbres, while inmates who perhaps should have been weren't. We had an inmate named James Allridge, who was on death row for murdering a convenience store clerk in Fort Worth in 1985. Allridge corresponded with the actress Susan Sarandon for years, and she even came to visit him a couple of weeks before his execution. Because I was the only woman around, they got me to walk her in and she bought some of his artwork. It never made sense to me. Allridge and his brother, who was also executed, went on a crime spree that resulted in the deaths of at least three people. Yes, Allridge had earned himself a degree in prison, but so had other people. And why did Gary Graham get all that attention? He was not a sympathetic character. He should not have been a poster child for the abolition movement. He, too, had gone on a horrible crime spree, robbing 13 different victims in nine different locations in less than a week. Two of his victims were pistol-whipped, another was shot in the neck, another was struck by the vehicle Graham was stealing from him. His final victim, Lisa Blackburn, was kidnapped, robbed and raped repeatedly over a period of five hours. None of this is disputed, because Graham pleaded guilty to all charges. The only crime he claimed he was falsely convicted of was the murder of Bobby Lambert at the start of his rampage.

Graham's argument was that he was convicted on the testimony of a single eyewitness. But that single eyewitness was black, like him, so it was difficult for his supporters to make it about race. Graham burned through 20 appeals in almost 19 years, which were reviewed by 33 judges and all of which were rejected, and was granted four stays of execution. But despite being under intense pressure, from all over the world, Governor Bush wouldn't yield. Bush's support for the death penalty carried no political risk, given that about two-thirds of Americans supported it. But Bush wasn't responsible for the spate of executions anyway, because the dates were set by the courts. And he couldn't have intervened in the case of Graham, because the Governor has very limited capabilities when it comes to stopping an execution. He or she can only grant a one-time, 30-day reprieve – anything else, including a longer stay or commutation of sentence, requires a recommendation from the

Texas Board of Pardons and Paroles, and Graham had already been reprieved once by a previous governor.

I'd interviewed Graham and I liked him. He talked a big game, said he'd fight to the death, but I got the sense he was just another guy on death row who was afraid to die. I'm not even sure he bought into everything he said and did, for example about his links to the New Black Panthers and changing his name 'to reflect his African heritage'. He was the kind of guy who claimed he was on a hunger strike and yet actually gained weight. To most inmates on death row, a hunger strike meant that every time the prison system brought them a meal they turned it down – but they still ate commissary. In other words, 'I rejected the breakfast you bastards offered me – but I then ate six Twinkies in my cell'.

While almost every right-minded person thought Graham was guilty, he managed to attract plenty of celebrity backers. Danny Glover and Spike Lee were vocal in their support, and Kenny Rogers offered to pay for a retrial. On the day of Graham's execution, Bianca Jagger and the Reverends Jesse Jackson and Al Sharpton turned up as witnesses. I think Graham was a pawn for the activists. It was a perfect relationship: he wanted someone to save him and they needed someone to further their cause. Once the celebrities were on board, the media piled in. And where there are cameras, there are people wanting to wave placards and make themselves heard.

'Exciting' isn't the word to describe the day of Gary Graham's execution. It was nuts, a little bit scary and probably the longest day of my entire life. I arrived at the Walls Unit at about 7 a.m. and there were hundreds of media already there, the whole parking lot was nothing but satellite trucks and journalists. The protesters started showing up about lunchtime, including the New Black Panthers, who were toting AK47s, and the Ku Klux Klan, in their hoods and robes. As you're probably aware, the Panthers and the KKK don't get along too well. Jesse Jackson kept trying to get on the podium, to speak to 'his people', and Larry had to tell him to speak to his people on the street. There was a Texas Department of Criminal Justice shield on that podium, and if Larry had let Jackson stand behind it, he'd have had the KKK asking if they could get up there and speak as well.

The police managed to keep the Panthers and the KKK a block apart, until the Panthers started marching around the other side of the block, along a street where there were no barricades. So now there were Panthers advancing towards the KKK and police and journalists running after the Panthers. It felt like it was about 300 degrees, there were helicopters hovering overhead, SWAT teams standing by, everybody was miserable and angry, and it felt like the whole thing might blow up at any moment. It was a fucking zoo.

Larry had had the building across from the Walls Unit fitted with tons of sockets so that reporters could plug in their computers and file their stories. So there we all were, typing away, when we heard this loud whirring sound. Everybody looked up, and there was Geraldo Rivera's lobster-red assistant, burned by the unforgiving

Texas sun, removing sweat from the tiny talk show host's hair with a fucking blow dryer. Geraldo was actually a likeable little man, but when lobster lady was blowing him down, I wanted to kick both their asses. Even more so when we found out Graham's lawyers had mounted last-ditch appeals, which delayed the execution by more than two hours. That's not to say those hours were just spent waiting – the scene outside was utter chaos. From the doorway outside Larry's office, I saw a warden get hit on the head with a bottle, a guy try to break through the barricade and get tackled to the ground by police officers, and somebody burning an American flag. And I wanted to be out there, where the action was.

Larry Fitzgerald

I remember one offender from Fort Worth saying, right before his execution, 'I'm gonna fight you, it's just my nature.' And when they tried to get him out of the holding cell, he was true to his word. With Gary Graham, they tried to surprise him and remove him from death row a day early. But Graham still put up a hell of a fight, just like he said he would. I rode over with the DPS sergeant, and I've never travelled so fast in a car in my life, because they thought the New Black Panthers might try to hijack the transport. Officers were literally sitting on Graham the entire way from Livingston to Huntsville.

I thought that when we got him to the death house, he'd be like a pussy cat, that perhaps he'd only fought on death row as an example to his offender buddies. They put him in a special cell, with no bunk or table, which he wasn't very happy about, and when they swung the cell door open, he fought like a tiger, more than any other offender I ever saw. The funny thing was, I was glad he did, because I'd been afraid that if I went out there after he'd been executed and said, 'Oh no, he didn't struggle', the media and his supporters would have called me a liar.

The extraction team, five of the biggest correctional officers I'd ever seen, went in with a shield, and managed to push him against the wall. At one point, I thought he was going to get away, but they managed to restrain him. Then they did something I'd never seen them do before: as well as straps, they put handcuffs on his hands and feet, because that was the only way they could get him on the gurney...

I find it hard to believe that if I was ever sentenced to death, I wouldn't put up a fight. I'd be biting and kicking and screaming and doing everything in my power to prevent them from getting me out of that holding cell. But hardly any of the inmates struggled. Almost all of them walked freely into the death chamber and popped right up there on the gurney, before stretching out their arms to receive the IV lines. That was the craziest thing to me, I just couldn't imagine being that resigned to my own death. Either they had lost their instinct to fight after all those years on death row, or they just wanted to take their punishment like a man. I honestly don't know. So when I heard that Graham had fought like hell, I had to give him some credit.

When the time came for Graham to give his last statement, they let him ramble on for 23 minutes. I think the warden was afraid to cut him short, because of his celebrity guests, who were in the witness room with me. I thought he was going to talk until midnight, which was when his death warrant would have expired. Graham's last words were: 'Keep marching, black people. They are murdering me tonight.' He died with one eye open and one eye closed, staring straight at the Reverend Jackson.

While we waited for the doctor, Jackson and Sharpton took turns saying prayers, while Jagger wept. At 8:49 p.m., Graham was pronounced dead, and I headed back to the newsroom to craft my final story. My day had begun at around 7 a.m. and it was after midnight when I finally got home. I felt truly exhausted, right down to my soul. It wasn't the hours, or the heat, or that I felt conflicted about his execution, because I did not. There was just so much drama and tension. All day, news was breaking all around us, so we had to remain vigilant. That was the most stressful execution I ever experienced.

The following morning, I was booked for an early interview with Katie Couric on *The Today Show*, which was a pretty big deal. All week, various friends had been messing around with Graham's name, in the hope of getting into my head. People were calling him Shaka Shakur, or Shaka Sleeper Sofa, lots of irreverent bullshit like that. And, sure enough, when Couric asked me about Graham's burial arrangements, I said his family planned to bury him under his African name, Shaka Shakur – as in Tupac. But that wasn't the worst part. First of all, when I listened to it back, I sounded like the biggest hick ever – like Clarice Starling in *The Silence of the Lambs*. I think that's when I started consciously thinking, 'If I want to be taken more seriously, I really need to start losing this Texas accent.' Then my friend called me and said, 'Congratulations, you're gonna win the award for biggest bitch in America. Because when Katie Couric asked if you had a hard time watching Gary Graham die, your response was a breezy, "No, not really."' I hadn't meant it to come across that way. That was me trying to say, 'I'm a journalist, and this is just what I do.' I was just young, you could hear that in my little girl Texas voice: I sounded like a child.

After that interview, I got lots of emails from people, some who supported the death penalty and thought I was doing a good job, some who were against the death penalty and thought I was awful, and some who were hitting on me ('both my friends and I thought Ms. Lyons was very pretty...'), which was flattering and creepy, all at the same time.

A week later, Jessy San Miguel was executed for shooting to death Michael Phelan, the manager of a Taco Bell restaurant in Irving, and possibly three others. There were maybe a dozen anti-death penalty protesters outside the Walls Unit as San Miguel was led to his death. Jackson, Sharpton and Jagger apparently had more pressing engagements. As he lay strapped to the gurney, with his arms outstretched as if attached to a crucifix, San Miguel said, 'Isn't it ironic? I'm a cross...'

CHAPTER 3
A FORK IN THE ROAD

'... the dignity of human life must never be taken away, even in the case of someone who has done great evil... the death penalty is both cruel and unnecessary.'

Pope John Paul II

'I think that the Pope and foreign countries should mind their own business. They need to worry about their own problems and leave Texas death row alone...'

Larry Wilkerson, husband of Glen McGinnis victim Leta Ann Wilkerson

On the day of an execution, I'd get to the Walls Unit at around 5 p.m. and head straight to Larry's office, where all the reporters would assemble. In Larry's office was a big couch, a table and two chairs, and one of those was set aside for Mike Graczyk from the Associated Press, who had been reporting on executions since 1984. I'd sit on the couch and listen to Larry holding court while leaning back in his chair with his boots on his desk.

There was a lot of gallows humour, which was irreverent, but not meant to be disrespectful. Larry would sometimes run a pool, where we'd try to predict the time of death. We'd make up joke headlines and think of songs to suit the occasion (for example, I still have a list Larry made before the execution of an inmate with one leg, including the songs 'Lean on Me' and 'You'll Never Walk Alone'). Graczyk made it his mission to make me laugh as we were entering the death chamber, because he knew it was such a fear of mine that I would. Maybe it was inappropriate, but it was just a coping mechanism, albeit a subconscious one.

There were also private jokes: Larry and Graczyk referred to the Texas prison system as 'the free world's largest gulag'.

Whenever Graczyk wrote up an interview, he would always try to use the line, 'the inmate said from a tiny visiting cage', just to ruffle Larry's feathers. Nobody ever discussed the rights or wrongs of an execution, it never got too heavy, because everybody knew what they were about to do, which was watch someone die and bear witness to their soul leaving their body. I'm told they only got burned once, just before I took over the prison beat, when it was Graczyk's birthday and Larry brought in a cake. A reporter from the *Daily Mail* in the UK portrayed it as if nobody gave a crap about what they were doing and were only interested in partying, which was obviously bullshit. After that, Larry was a lot more careful about who to be real around.

> 'Caldwell initially told police he accidentally killed his parents and sister after they each ran into his knife during an argument. Former Dallas County assistant prosecutor Andy Beach said the statement was remembered as the "magic knife confession". We joked that Caldwell was going to have a run-in with the "magic needle".'
>
> **Michelle's journal, on the execution of Jeffery Caldwell, 30 August 2000**

It was important we had that time in Larry's office before an execution, because afterwards it was business. The victim's family would often choose to hold a press conference, at which the TV journalists would annoy the crap out of us with the same two stupid questions: 'Does this bring you closure?' and 'Do you feel justice has been served?' Us newspaper journalists would look at each other and roll our eyes. We knew they were stupid questions, because the answers would always be the same: 'No, it doesn't bring us closure, because it doesn't bring our loved ones back. It's the end of the chapter, we're glad it happened, but it doesn't change anything.' As for the second question, it was always a yes or no answer.

Graczyk would always ask the same question, but it was a brilliant one: 'Are you glad you came?' Technically, it's a yes or no answer. But they hardly ever said 'no', and nobody ever left it at 'yes'.

'It's hard to put anybody to death as violently as Tommy Ray Jackson put my daughter to death. It's enough that he was put to death. But I think "Old Sparky" put on a better show.'

Dr Roger Robison, father of Rosalind Robison, murdered by Tommy Ray Jackson. Jackson was executed on 4 May 2000

Back in Larry's office, we'd come to a consensus as to what was said in the inmate's last statement, because the official TDCJ version would often be wrong – not just the odd word missing, but entire sentences – and get down to writing our stories. Did he look at the victim's family and apologise? Did he ignore the victim's family and speak to his own? What did members of the victim's family say? What did the prosecutor say? What was his last meal?

None of us spoke to each other about what we'd just seen in serious terms. Larry was a spokesman for the prison system, so it would have been inappropriate for him to tell anyone how he felt about the death penalty. It would have been inappropriate for me to talk about it because, as a journalist, I was supposed to be neutral. It wasn't uncommon for me, some of the correctional officers, Larry and Chaplain Brazzil – who Larry nicknamed 'The Sinister Minister', or 'Sinister' for short, because when Brazzil paid you a visit, you knew you were in trouble – to go for cocktails after we'd filed our stories. I was usually the only girl there and we'd drink, as Larry liked to say, copious amounts of alcohol (except for Brazzil, who abstained). It's not as if we'd be dancing on tables, but we'd sit around, tell stories, make fun of each other, and talk about anything other than executions. I was a kid, enjoying life. Brazzil once asked if watching men die bothered me, and I replied, 'No, it really doesn't.' And because I didn't think anybody else wanted to get deep, I never asked them if they were struggling with it either.

Larry Fitzgerald

I was very apprehensive before my first execution. Wouldn't you feel nervous if you were about to see somebody executed for the first time? In the days leading up to it, I had kind of an empty feeling, because I just didn't know what to expect. Was the offender going to be violent? Was he going to be sick? Would he start pleading for his life?

I walked into the witness room and thought, 'By the time I walk out of here, somebody's gonna be dead.' I saw the offender on the gurney, a guy out of Taylor County by the name of Clifton Russell Jr, the chemicals hit and that was it. It was so clinical, like watching an ER operation, only where the patient dies. And it was so quick, over in a matter of minutes. My initial reaction was, 'Is that all there is to that?' As a reporter, I'd seen people shot and cut up, so watching someone be executed seemed pretty genteel in comparison. Half an hour later, I was back in there to witness Willie Williams of Harris County go through the same process.

At that time, we were executing people starting at midnight, and the second execution finished at about 4 a.m. I went home, grabbed an hour of sleep, then had to go back to my office to catch the early news cycle. I thought I was in the wrong job, watching men die in the middle of the night. A few months later, they changed things so that executions started at 6 p.m. But I didn't like watching men die any better, it was horrible. I remember one offender, he was black, and everyone in the witness rooms was white. I thought, 'Here's this black guy strapped to the gurney, and he's looking over to see all these white faces looking back at him.' That bothered me.

During that period when so many offenders were being sent to the death chamber under Governor Bush, I became the face of executions in Texas, and executions became routine to me. After you've seen a bunch of executions, you can almost set your watch by them. Most of the offenders I saw executed were soon just names on a page, and it bothered me that I could stand there, watch somebody's life being taken by the state – which is the ultimate bureaucratic act – walk out of that room and forget about it. But I think that was my way of coping with what I'd seen. If I'd carried the burden of every execution I saw, I'd have gone crazy in no time.

I really started having doubts about what I was doing about four years in. I started to question an offender's guilt, which is something I never should have done. And I started thinking we might have executed people we shouldn't have. For example, I had doubts about David Spence, who was executed for the infamous Lake Waco murders, when three teenagers were stabbed to death in 1982. Spence was convicted largely because of the testimony of prison inmates, and various investigations suggested he wasn't a part of it. I also thought we were executing people who were mentally unstable, like Monty Delk, who I thought was crazy as a peach orchard boar, but the authorities thought was faking it.

There was a feeling of helplessness, standing behind the glass and thinking those things. What could I do about it? Not a thing. It was just part of the job I signed up for. Someone committed a murder, they were executed, and it just happened that I was there. Or at least that's how I had to think of it. A warden once said to me, 'Once you've seen an execution, you can never go back.' He was right, I couldn't.

But my biggest problem was becoming too close with offenders. When death row was at the Ellis Unit, it was how you would picture a prison out of a Hollywood movie. The cells had bars and they'd have what they called 'in and out', when they would roll the cell doors and the offenders would have some recreation time on the wing. I'd sit on their bunks and talk to them. These were convicted murderers, but I never once felt threatened. I always felt safe on death row, because offenders realised I was their conduit to the media, and therefore the outside world. I wasn't a correctional officer, I wasn't a warden, I was somebody entirely different.

When death row was at Ellis, they had work programmes as an incentive for good behaviour. Some of the inmates worked on the painting crew, others worked in a garment factory, making uniforms for correctional officers. They only made one part of the uniform, otherwise the inmates would have got all dressed up as COs and walked right out of there. The factory was air-conditioned, the inmates could smoke and had access to coffee. It was also a place to socialise. Some of the most notorious offenders in Texas were in that garment factory, and there would be all sorts of tools lying around, but I'd walk in there and chew the fat with them.

They liked the fact I treated them like human beings. I got my shoes shined in prison, my shirts cleaned and pressed. I'd sit and watch The Golden Girls with the inmates while I was having my hair cut. It kept the inmates active, and it was cheap. I'd leave cigarettes and chilli sauce outside my apartment, for inmates on the trash crew to find. If an inmate didn't have money for the bus after he'd been released, I'd give him some. An inmate named Arnold Darby made my boots. When he finally got out, after 37 years inside, I endeavoured to set him up with work, but he couldn't handle the outside world, and was soon back inside again. But at least I tried.

There was a guy on death row called Jermarr Arnold, who every officer was afraid of. He was a huge man, could have played in the NFL. Arnold killed a jewellery store clerk in Corpus Christi, fled to California and wound up in Pelican Bay, which was a notoriously bad penitentiary. In fact, it was so bad that Arnold confessed to the killing in Corpus Christi, because he thought he'd be safer on Texas death row. One time, I was sitting in the warden's office at Polunsky and they brought him in in shackles. He said to me, 'Mr Fitzgerald, they don't need to shackle me with you, I like you.' We had a nice conversation and left on a friendly note. Before they executed him, he requested that nobody witness him leaving death row, so Michelle and I were told to hide around a corner. As I recall, Arnold went to his death without any struggle at all.

Arnold got a guy named Emerson Rudd to kill a fellow inmate in the rec yard at the Ellis Unit, by driving a screwdriver through his temple. When Emerson got his execution date, he was in the search area and they had to put him in a little cage, in case he wanted to fight anybody. He refused to come out, so they gassed him – and, man, did they gas him, his skin was red raw when they dragged him out of that place. They slapped him on a gurney, and as he rolled past me, he looked over and gave me a thumbs-up. Call it Stockholm syndrome, call it what you want, but I liked Emerson a lot.

Offenders would tell me stories about their mothers and fathers and kids. If they wanted to talk about their crime, sure, I'd sit there and listen to them. But I made it a point not to bring it up, because I didn't think it was any of my business. I soon learned that while a lot of death row offenders had committed really horrible crimes, they were still people. There was often drugs or drink involved, they'd got themselves into a bad situation or made a bad career choice.

Karla Faye Tucker murdered two people with a pickaxe in Houston in 1983 while high on speed and liquor. When the bodies were discovered, the girl still had the pickaxe embedded in her chest. But I was fond of Karla Faye, and I think she was fond of me. She was a born-again Christian, and I had no reason to doubt her sincerity. I'm aware of that old saying that there are no atheists in fox holes, but she had a spirituality about her. She even married a prison minister. As far as I was concerned, she was a good person who made a terrible mistake. Brazzil told me that he had 18 guys come to his office at the Walls Unit and say, 'Chaplain, please let me take her place on the gurney.' She made that kind of impact on people. I always said that if Karla Faye ever got off death row, she could move in next door to me.

Before I arrived at TDCJ, female death row in Gatesville was a real closed community and they wouldn't do any media. But I got them to open up. Frances Newton, who was convicted of killing her husband and two small children in 1987, knitted a blanket for my mother. It had yellow roses on it, because my mother was a Yellow Rose of Texas. Frances was a good person, I liked her a lot, as I liked most of the inmates on female death row.

Just before her execution, Karla Faye said, 'Mr Fitzgerald, you've never lied to me before. What are they gonna do to me tonight?'

I said, 'They're gonna kill you, Karla Faye.'

She laughed and said, 'I knew that.'

That was the last conversation I had with her. Karla Faye's execution was another celebrity affair, with an extraordinary amount of media attention, because she was female and an axe murderer. There were hundreds of anti-death penalty protesters outside the Walls Unit, but also lots of people for it. When news reached them that Karla Faye was dead, they started cheering.

Karla Faye's last meal was a banana, a peach and a garden salad. She truly was not afraid of being executed, she literally skipped down the hall to the death chamber, because she was convinced she was going to a better place. But I was pretty moved by her execution. I hated seeing her on that gurney, it drove me up the wall.

James Beathard was involved in a triple-murder in Trinity County in 1984. He always protested his innocence, but it didn't matter to me one way or the other. On the afternoon of his execution, I asked him if there was anything I could do for him, and he said, 'I'd really like some bing cherries.' Lucky for him, bing cherries were in season. So I got myself down to the grocery store, bought a couple of pounds of bing cherries, and we sat there in the death house eating them together. A few hours later, I was watching through the glass as he was lying on the gurney. I thought of past conversations I'd had with him, about the laughs we'd shared and the fact that, in a few moments, he was going to be dead. These weren't people they just picked off the street and executed, these were friends of mine.

I was sober for a period of five and a half years after my stint at Alcoholics Anonymous. I was drinking again by the time I started working for the prison system, but watching all those executions made me want to drink more. After Gary Graham's execution, I cried in the car on the way home, before crawling into a bottle of Scotch. People calling you a murderer will do that to you.

I had two crutches: whisky and Jim Brazzil. Brazzil was a very gregarious person and I just fell in love with him as soon as I met him. I always used to say I spent half my life in Huntsville and my best friend was a Baptist preacher, that's how dull my life was. But The Sinister Minister was one hell of a guy, and absolutely genuine. Warner Brothers offered $2.5 million to base a television series on him, and he turned it down. He didn't want to cheapen his role, which was to glorify God.

Me and Brazzil would sometimes talk on the phone late into the night about executions. He'd be drinking Dr Pepper and I'd be drinking liquor. I thought Brazzil had the toughest job in the whole place. On the day of an execution, he'd spend three hours with the offender, between three and six o'clock, trying to get their spiritual house in order. He made my job a lot easier, because of his openness and the rapport he had with offenders. He also presided over some of their funerals and ministered to prison staff. I provided a release for him, and he provided a release for me. It was like we were counselling each other, only he was more qualified than I was.

There is another guy who springs to mind, who stabbed two women to death in Austin in 1986, while high on Jack Daniel's and pills.

I remember his crime well, because it happened down the street from where I went to high school. It troubles me that I don't remember his name. We grew to like each other, and when he was in the holding cell getting ready for his execution, he said to me, 'Well, Larry, you knew it was gonna to come down to this sooner or later.'

I recall that the musician Steve Earle, who the offender had corresponded with, was there to witness. But there were no rock songs on the gurney. The offender was a very serious Catholic, and when he was on the gurney, he recited this long passage from Corinthians, the one that begins, 'And now I will show you the most excellent way'. He had agreed with Brazzil and the warden that once he'd finished preaching and started singing 'Silent Night', the lethal dose would be administered...

'Silent Night,

'Holy Night,

'All is calm,

'All is bright,

'Round yon Virgin...'

That's how long it takes for a man to die in Texas. Christmas was never the same...

The prison beat wasn't just about witnessing executions, that was only a small part of the job. With that many prisons in the city, you never knew what was going to happen when you woke up in the morning. Was there going to be an escape? Was there going to be a hostage situation? Was an officer going to be stabbed or murdered?

In my previous job, I'd been covering Huntsville City Council meetings, which generally weren't too exciting. On the prison beat, there were always crazy things going on. As well as spot news and trials arising from attacks on officers, I covered administrative stuff. If TDCJ had a new director, I'd interview him and find out what his vision was. During the legislative session, when it was time for TDCJ to set its budget and discuss issues and initiatives, I'd attend board meetings, not just in Huntsville but all over the state. One month, a meeting might be in Dallas, the next it might be in McAllen, which is eight or nine hours away. Texas is a damn big place.

I'd also interview inmates on death row, usually if they had an execution date. There were some inmates who would not talk to journalists at all. Usually it was because they didn't trust the media, but others were advised by their lawyers not to. I put in a few requests to interview Betty Lou Beets, the so-called 'Black Widow', who buried husbands in her garden as if they were dead pets. She eventually agreed but, having driven the two and half hours to women's death row in Gatesville, she declined me at the last minute. That was kind of rude of her. Consequently, the first time I saw her was when she was laid out on the gurney. She was tiny, and I remember thinking, 'She looks like a little old grandma. Wait a second, she is a little old grandma...' But I never heard her speak, because she declined to make a last statement.

But a lot of times the inmates did speak to me. Why wouldn't they? They were locked in their cells for 23 hours a day, and here was a chance to have a degree of intimacy with another human being, albeit through a sheet of Plexiglass. Not only that, these were desperate men who mistakenly thought we might be able to help their case.

One of the condemned men I interviewed was Napoleon Beazley. On 19 April 1994, Napoleon and some friends carjacked an elderly couple in the city of Tyler, 130 miles north of Houston. Napoleon was only 17. They followed the couple to their home and when they pulled into their garage, Napoleon and his friends attacked them and shot the man to death. The man's wife played dead on the floor, before Napoleon and his friends took off in their prize, a 10-year-old Mercedes-Benz. Napoleon had picked the wrong victims. The couple's son was a federal judge, J. Michael Luttig, which made the death penalty almost inevitable, at least for whoever pulled the trigger.

Napoleon played for his high school football team, was class president, good-looking, personable and had lots of friends. His parents were upstanding members of the community, with a big house in the small town of Grapeland, about 130 miles north of Houston. Up until the night he decided to murder John Luttig, Napoleon seemed to have led a charmed existence. But 47 days after his crime, and two weeks after graduating 13th from his class of 60, a tip led the police to Grapeland and Napoleon was arrested and charged with murder. The following year, Napoleon was sentenced to death. His two accomplices, Cedric and Donald Coleman, testified against him and were given life sentences.

Because of his age at the time of the crime, Napoleon's case drew international attention. Texas was one of 22 states that allowed the death penalty for defendants 17 or older (17 states allowed it for 16-year-olds), but Napoleon's lawyers and anti-death penalty activists lobbied the Governor and appealed to the US Supreme Court and the Texas Board of Pardons and Paroles. Clemency pleas rained down from the European Union, Archbishop Desmond Tutu, the American Bar Association, the judge who presided over Napoleon's capital murder trial and the district attorney in Napoleon's home county. Amnesty International pointed out that the United States was one of only five countries to execute 'juveniles', the others being Saudi Arabia, Iran, Congo and Nigeria. Napoleon's supporters also pointed out that he had no previous convictions, was a black man tried by an all-white jury, and that the death penalty was sought against him because of the victim's judicial ties.

Napoleon was a light-skinned black man who felt like he didn't fit in – he wasn't white enough to feel at home in the white community and he wasn't black enough to feel at home in the black community, some of whom mocked him for his erudition and the way he spoke. As a result, he started running with a rougher crowd – black kids who carried guns and dealt drugs – to prove he belonged. When I spoke to Napoleon a couple of weeks before his execution date, as was my routine, my first impressions were that he was very articulate, very smart, a nice kid who fell in with some bad people. It was seven years since he'd murdered John Luttig, and he seemed to be a completely different person to how he was portrayed in the court filings and trial.

We were about the same age and his upbringing hadn't been too different to mine, but that wasn't necessarily why I empathised with him. When I was a freshman at Texas A&M, there was a guy who stalked a fellow student, broke into her apartment and killed her, before setting the apartment on fire to cover up evidence. He was fine to talk to when I met him on death row, polite and respectful, but I didn't feel sorry for him at all. There were plenty of other guys who were extremely articulate on death row, and it wasn't necessarily indicative of their education – most of them were done with school after eighth grade – but sometimes I got the overwhelming sense that they were bullshitting me. They'd tell me they were innocent, despite all the evidence to the contrary. That bothered me; I'd just want them to own it and stop wasting everyone's time. I also understood why, because they just didn't want to die. But that's not how Napoleon came across. He was particularly insightful, very sincere and made no bones about what he had done. After interviewing him, I thought, 'If this guy wasn't on death row, we might even be friends.'

> 'I imagine [being on death row] is like a cancer. It eats away at you piece by piece, and then you get to a point where you don't care if you live or die. It's possible I'll get a stay of execution, but it's not likely. It's like a hole-in-one in golf.'
>
> **Napoleon Beazley, as quoted in Michelle's story in *The Huntsville Item*, 15 August 2001**

I quickly became aware that pretty much the whole world beyond America thought it was weird that we were still putting people to death. I cannot tell you how many interviews I gave and stories that were written about me – in Germany, France, Spain, Australia – because I was this young woman watching all these executions. And I could tell immediately what their angle was, because European journalists would often use the word 'killing' instead of 'executing'. That's how they viewed it, that we were murdering someone, and I would feel the need to correct them. It would bug me, because it showed bias and a lack of empathy on their part.

The German director Werner Herzog made a film about life on death row, and what I liked about him was that although he was staunchly anti-death penalty, that wasn't his angle. He didn't even care if the inmates he spoke to claimed to be innocent, he was only interested in how inmates prepared mentally for an execution. I respected him for that, and he wasn't the only European who took an even-handed approach to coverage of the death penalty. But a lot of European journalists weren't so impartial. I'd watch them in the interview room, with their hands on the glass, and think, 'Will you knock that shit off, that's what families do. You don't even know him…' It upset Larry sometimes, made him really angry. After Gary Graham's execution, an Italian journalist, a woman, ran up to him and screamed in his face, 'The culture of death! The culture of death!' Larry was standing on the steps in front of the Walls Unit, just wanting to go home after a particularly trying day at work. He used to say to me, 'These people have come here with an agenda, and they're supposed to be reporters…'

In the weeks leading up to Napoleon's scheduled execution, I got a ton of letters and emails from all over the world. Some were downright creepy. There was one guy from Germany who was relentless. In one email, he told me he'd had a dream in which he'd been very naughty and I'd had to spank him. I got the Office of Inspector General involved and it turned out this guy worked for Siemens, although I got the feeling the other spelling was also involved. He even called the *Item* and asked for my father, because he was trying to establish if I was married or not and thought David Lyons might be my husband.

But mostly the letters and emails concerned the death penalty. Some were supportive, but most were scathing, especially from people in Europe. It would floor me when I got an email from someone in, for example, Sweden, telling me what an awful person I was. It drove me nuts. For a while, I took it. But then I stopped taking it and started writing back, to the extent that sometimes I would be kind of nasty. I was young, had less patience and self-control, but I was also desperate to present the other side of the argument. My reaction back then was to fight my corner: 'How dare you criticise us and our justice system? What do you know about anything in Texas anyway?' There was no middle ground with me, although I was more considered when I produced an article for the *Item* defending my role, in which I wrote: '"How can you stand to watch men die?" It's a question I get quite a bit. And the funny thing is, I don't think I've gotten any better at crafting a clever response. I never will be able to say I enjoy watching a man take his last breath. I do it because it's my job.'

It wasn't just foreigners who didn't understand what we were doing. *Rolling Stone* published an ugly article in which they destroyed Huntsville, and Larry in particular. The writer called Larry 'a boob' – and much worse – and called for Governor Bush to sack him. He called me 'the young Texas A&M graduate who has seen more death than can be healthy for someone her age'. It was extremely condescending and made me angry. I was busting my ass to be every bit as good as any other reporter, and that's how I was described. Christiane Amanpour also wielded the hatchet when she did a big piece about Napoleon for CNN. Larry was showing her the holding cell and explaining that if a condemned man hadn't requested a last meal, they would put out snacks and punch, in case he got hungry. He described it as a 'party platter', and Amanpour said, 'Oh, because it's a *party*?' Larry didn't mean it like that.

Amanpour was something else. When she interviewed me, she called me 'a cub reporter' and said, 'Isn't it strange, a young woman watching all this death?' That made me angry, because although I was young, I had about seven years' experience behind me as a journalist. What made me angrier was the fact that she was a female reporter as well, who had been covering conflicts since her early twenties. I could have said the same thing to her: 'Was it appropriate for you to be covering the Iran–Iraq War, wearing your ridiculous safari jacket, when it's 300 fucking degrees outside?' For the longest time, whenever somebody mentioned Christiane Amanpour, I'd say, '*Fuck* Christiane Amanpour!'

I witnessed 38 of the 40 executions carried out in Texas in 2000, missing two because I was covering prison board meetings. I don't remember thinking we were executing too many people. It was bizarre, because we'd never seen anything like it before. But I was more concerned about the fact we had too much crime.

People say everything is bigger in Texas – it's a place where you can order burgers in restaurants with two doughnuts instead of a bun – and maybe that extends to crime. Certainly, Texas crime seemed crazier than in other states. Take Lisa Nowak, a Houston astronaut who drove 900 miles to Florida – while allegedly wearing a 'space diaper' – to confront a woman who was dating her ex. This was a very smart woman – she worked for NASA, for God's sake – and she tried to kidnap this random chick, pepper sprayed her in an airport parking lot. That's why Larry loved doing radio in Fort Worth, because Fort Worth had a reputation for crazy crime, even as far as Texas was concerned.

In Texas, you get home from work, turn on the news and there are always stories of random shootings, stabbings and rapes. It's every day and it's awful. One woman witnessed two executions that I saw in 2001 – Jack Wade Clark and Adolph Hernandez – because in two unrelated cases Clark killed her daughter and Hernandez killed her mom, within a year of each other. The death penalty was a symptom of all that crime. On top of that, because crime is so well documented in America, in terms of newspaper and magazine features and websites, documentaries and movies, it becomes this great, amorphous mass. To illustrate, I had a poster from the set of *The Life of David Gale* pinned up in my office, and one day a TV reporter came in and said, 'Whoa, David Gale, I remember that case. That was a huge one, they don't come much bigger than that.' I nodded, but must have looked at her as if she were crazy, because *The Life of David Gale* was entirely fictional and the guy on the poster was the actor Kevin Spacey.

It's not that witnessing executions had become mundane, and therefore normal – watching the final moments of someone's life and their soul leave their body never becomes mundane or normal – but Texas was putting people to death with such frequency that it had perfected it, and therefore removed the theatre. Lethal injection doesn't have the drama of hanging or firing squad or 'Old Sparky'. Execution in Texas was a clinical process; there was even a certain decorum about it, what with the chaplain placing his hand on the inmate's knee and the warden making sure a pillow was in place on the gurney. On 12 June 2000, after the execution of Thomas Mason, I wrote in my journal: 'He lay there, looking like an old man who had fallen asleep in his armchair, with his mouth slightly agape.' It was Mason as my grandpa again, doing nothing more dramatic than taking an early evening nap.

Therefore, there came a time when they all started merging into one. When you execute that many people, most of them cease to be events. Gary Graham might have generated thousands of column inches all over the world, but when Daniel Hittle was executed on 6 December 2000 for killing a police officer and four other people, including a four-year-old, not one reporter from the Dallas area, where the crime took place, came to witness. Like Larry said one time, 'One day we've got crowds out there and they're proclaiming, by God, it's such a horrible thing. And the next time, I could shoot a cannon down the street and not hit anybody.'

After Jack Wade Clark was executed on 9 January 2001, I wrote one sentence in my journal, a brief description of his crime, and stopped. That was my last ever entry. I'm very organised, a big list person, and I think that journal was my way of compartmentalising the executions, separating them from the rest of my life. But maybe I realised, on a subconscious level, that even revisiting my feelings about executions and writing them down was dangerous. It's as if I was standing at a fork in the road and decided to take a safer route.

That was the point at which I started stowing my thoughts in a mental suitcase – and not folding them up neatly beforehand, but scrunching them up and flinging them in. As far as my job went, it didn't matter what I felt, all that mattered was what an inmate did to be up on that gurney and what happened when he was on there, which I wrote about in dry prose for *The Huntsville Item*. Nobody would have thought watching all those executions was affecting me, which was why nobody felt the need to ask if I was coping okay. Even I didn't think watching all those executions was affecting me, I thought I was absolutely fine.

CHAPTER 4
THAT'S JUST LARRY

'When's the last time we burned someone at the stake? It's been too long! Put it on TV on Sunday mornings... You don't think that would get big ratings? In this sick fucking country?! Shit, you'd have people skipping church to watch this stuff!'

George Carlin, American comedian

'I said I was going to tell a joke...'

The last statement of Patrick Knight, executed 26 June 2007

I loved being a reporter, and never thought I would leave journalism, even though the hours were shit and the money was worse. Because I worked hard at *The Huntsville Item* and wrote a ton of in-depth features, a lot of my stuff got picked up by the Associated Press and was sent out on the wires, which in turn led to job offers from bigger newspapers, such as *The Beaumont Enterprise*, the *Waco Tribune-Herald* and the *Galveston Daily News*. But I stayed at the *Item* because I hoped that if I kept writing in-depth prison stuff, I'd eventually get the opportunity to work for one of the really big newspapers, like the *Houston Chronicle* or *The Dallas Morning News*.

Then, towards the end of 2001, a spokesperson's job came up at TDCJ. I'd been offered a potential job at Sam Houston State and in an insurance office, which would have paid more money, but neither of them interested me. The job with TDCJ was the only job I would have left journalism for, because the prisons were so fascinating to me.

It helped that they were offering double what I was making as a journalist, and I'd become such good friends with Larry, and got to know his boss Larry Todd well.

When I was at the *Item*, Todd and Fitzgerald arranged for me to visit prison units all over the state, covering the prison system's various industries, and they would often come with me. One thing the Texas prison system was very good at was teaching inmates vocational skills, especially as they were approaching their release dates. At one unit, there was a garage where inmates repaired school buses. Those buses would get shipped down there from all over the state, and the inmates would learn mechanics and body repair and fix them up to look like new. Some inmates learned how to fix and rebuild old computers, which were then sent to low-income school districts across Texas. There was a mattress factory, which churned out all the mattresses the inmates slept on, as well as the students at state universities, including Texas A&M. My mattress came from that factory, although when I got him home I started thinking, 'You know what would be a genius way to escape from prison? Sew yourself inside a mattress...' That was the best mattress I ever had, but for the first couple of weeks, I kept imagining someone cutting themselves out in the middle of the night and attacking me. At another unit, they made braille books for the blind; at another, they made toys. Working for TDCJ is about the only public information job where you don't want a lot of media attention, because there's usually only media attention in the prison system when something bad happens. But these were good news stories, and I made that the thrust of my interview, that there needed to be more positivity and proactivity.

Todd had a TV background, Fitzgerald had a radio background, so they wanted a writer. They also wanted someone younger, preferably a woman, and thought it would help if the successful candidate spoke Spanish – my mom's family is Greek and Hispanic, so while my conversational Spanish mostly sucked, I understood it pretty well. They tailored the job description for me, decided that I'd aced my interview, and in November 2001, I cleared my desk at the *Item* and started in my new role at TDCJ.

A couple of weeks in, Fitzgerald said, 'I'm gonna take you to the Byrd Unit. It's important you see the classification process, we get a lot of questions about that.' The Byrd Unit is an intake facility in Huntsville, where male offenders enter the prison system. We showed up, met the warden, I followed Larry down a corridor, heard water running, and suddenly I was surrounded by about 40 naked men, showering and preparing to don their new prison garb. Larry looked at me and started laughing. I stared back, shook my head slightly and thought, 'You motherfucker.' I was determined to show it didn't bother me, but of course it bothered me, I was surrounded by 40 potentially dangerous and very naked men. I was terrified to look anywhere, in case one of them accused me of eyeing up their junk. With Larry it was all about tests, and he loved making me squirm.

Next, he marched me through all the different levels of administration segregation in the Estelle Unit's High Security building. 'Ad Seg' is where the worst of the death row inmates are housed, as well as inmates from the general population with behavioural problems. Offenders in Ad Seg are confined to their cell 23 hours a day and have very little interaction with fellow inmates. Most gang members are housed at level one, where they are segregated for their own safety, and it's eerily quiet in that cell block. Level two is more rowdy, and three is like a living nightmare, the most intimidating thing I ever saw in the prison system. The day Larry gave me his guided tour, one inmate was smearing his own faeces (at least I assume it was his own faeces) all over the window of his cell door.

Larry also made me eat 'food loaf', which is what inmates are given as a punishment if they start acting up and throwing their real food around. Food loaf is basically lots of food items blended into a glob. It's nutritious, but completely bland – like dry cornbread that needs a lot of salt. He claimed I had to eat it in case any reporters asked me how it tasted, which was, of course, bullshit. He did stuff like that all the time, had a very mischievous sense of humour.

Larry was child-like, but also very smart, and I think he saw me as a kindred spirit. He nicknamed me 'Little Larry', and I'd say, 'I'll come to the bar with you, but I'm not drinking Scotch or smoking those unfiltered cigarettes, and I'm definitely not growing a moustache.' My favourite poet is Dorothy Parker, but there aren't many people in Huntsville who'd know who she was. Larry knew immediately, and he sometimes called me 'Miss Parker'. Other times he'd call me 'Patches', from a song by Clarence Carter, which had the line, 'I was so ragged, the folks used to call me Patches.' Larry said to me, 'You're ragged, so I'm gonna call *you* Patches.' That was kind of mean, but it was Larry, so I loved it. He'd send me funny emails after a big night out, describing his hangover – 'Jesus, man, my breath could knock a buzzard off a shit wagon' – and another thing he loved to do was suddenly start using some huge, obscure word. Because I never pretended to know what it meant, he'd have to tell me and that would delight him. He loved words, and I swear he sat at his computer looking new ones up, just so he could try them out on me.

Larry Fitzgerald

There was a certain amount of gallows humour that went with the job. When you'd seen as many executions as we had, there had to be. One offender was going to fight, and a correctional officer said to him, 'You don't wanna fight, because if you do, you're gonna get scuffed up.' I thought that was the funniest statement – this guy was about to die, like he cared about getting scuffed up.

Officers were always good for a funny line. I was over on death row one day, and the major said to me, 'Hey, we're bringing Brewer in, do you wanna come back to the infirmary and take a look?' Lawrence Brewer was one of three white supremacists convicted of killing James Byrd, a black man, in Jasper in 1998. Brewer, Shawn Berry and John King dragged Byrd behind a pick-up truck for three miles, before dumping his decapitated body in front of an

African-American cemetery. Nothing funny so far. But when Brewer came in, they told him what to expect – he was going to be medically examined, they were going to take photos of his tattoos – and when they told him they were going to give him a few shots, he said, 'Oh man, I hate needles!' And the officer said, 'You've come to the wrong place, partner...'

Lesley Gosch and his accomplice murdered the wife of a bank president when an attempted kidnapping went wrong. He wore eyeglasses, and they were very, very thick, like the bottom of Coke bottles. He was essentially blind without those things, but the warden, in his wisdom, decided to remove them on the night of his execution. After the chemicals hit, the warden summoned the physician to check for signs of life. One of the exercises they do is to open an offender's eyes, and when the physician did so, one of them popped out. The physician caught it in mid-air and stuffed it back into the socket. Afterwards, he stormed into the warden's office, shouting, 'Why the hell did nobody tell me the convict had a glass eye?'

There was another gentleman we executed, an old, feeble black man, who had been on death row for so long that nobody turned up. Either everybody else involved with the crime had died off or they just didn't care, so it wound up that it was only myself and Graczyk in the witness room. The old man gave some real disjointed final statement, to the extent that we couldn't work out what he was saying, but as the chemicals started flowing, he strained against the straps and roared, 'How 'bout them Cowboys?' Boom, he was dead. The Dallas Cowboys *had played the night before and somehow managed to snatch victory from the jaws of defeat. Me and Graczyk looked at each other and couldn't help laughing.*

Joseph Faulder killed an elderly lady in a robbery in Gladewater, way back in 1975. Because Faulder was a Canadian citizen, he had a ton of appeals and was on death row for almost 25 years. Faulder and I got along real well, and when he received a last-minute stay of execution, I ran from my office to the death house to give him the good news. When I busted in, Brazzil asked me what I was doing there, and I said, 'Faulder, you got a stay!' He replied, 'Far out!' And I said, 'Faulder, how long have you been in here? Nobody has used that expression in 20 years.' After a long pause, he said, 'Let me ask you this, Mr Fitzgerald, when is your birthday?' I told him, and he said, 'Well, how about that, you're older than I am, turkey...' We all laughed, including Brazzil. The Sinister Minister took his job as a man of God very seriously, but laughter was as important to him as it was to me...

'Before Joseph Faulder was executed, Larry called me and said he needed me to do an interview with a Canadian television station. This young lady was interviewing me, I was getting pretty deep into the spiritual aspect of an execution, and she said, "I have one final question for you: I understand you have a very strong ministry at Rubber Ducky's, here in Huntsville. Would you care to elaborate on that?" Rubber

Ducky's was a sex shop in town. I blushed and said, "Have you been talking to that pervert Fitzgerald?" The young lady burst out laughing.

'I was being interviewed by this other lady, when all of a sudden I heard this great big noise. I thought it was her, and she thought it was me. A few minutes later, I heard another noise, this time a big, juicy one. When there was a third noise, I cracked: "Look, that's not me." She said, "Well, it's not me either." So I flipped over my chair and there was this fart box taped to the bottom. I could hear Larry in his office, dying with laughter...'

Jim Brazzil, former Huntsville Unit chaplain

Later, I got to hear stories about Larry's younger years, when he was as wild as the wind. When he was a student, he drilled a hole in the trunk of his car, filled the trunk with ice and rode around selling booze. Larry loved telling me, 'Students were lining up at my goddamned car every day for weeks.' When a landlord gave him permission to renovate an apartment, he painted the whole thing black, including the windows.

Larry was a rock and roll guy, spun music on the radio during the sixties and seventies, and had this free spirit. But he was very serious about his job at TDCJ, and very good at it. Larry knew what journalists wanted and taught me just about everything I know about being a public information officer. He knew how much access you needed to give to journalists and valued transparency. When Karla Faye Tucker was executed in 1998, the first woman to be put to death in Texas in the 20th century, the warden lied to him about her whereabouts beforehand, which he then relayed to the media. When Larry found out, he was livid. The journalists had come to expect the truth from Larry, and the warden had undermined his credibility. Larry knew you could not lie, which was never to be confused with telling the media everything. He used to call us 'the professional secret keepers'.

Because he was so good at his job, and so respected by journalists, he got away with plenty of things that anyone else would have been fired for. You'd hear people say all the time, 'Oh, that's just Fitzgerald…' There was an Italian reporter he hated, absolutely despised, and every time Larry saw him he flipped him the finger, while all the other journalists were looking. I've no doubt Larry also called him a 'cocksucker', because that was his favourite insult. There were two French reporters in town for another execution and it started raining. When they asked Larry if there was anywhere they could shelter, he replied, 'Quit moaning, this is probably the first bath you've had in ten years.' I'd be thinking, 'Larry! You're gonna get us into trouble!' It was a tobacco-free system, but he used to help sneak cigarettes to inmates who were due to be executed. You weren't allowed to smoke in state cars, but Larry was heavy-duty, and his ashtray would be spilling over with tons and tons of unfiltered cigarettes. All these newfangled rules just weren't for him.

One time, there was an escape, and Larry was in the car with the big boss director of the prison system and some other high-level officials. They stopped at a convenience store, for water and snacks, and Larry came back with a six-pack of beer. He didn't pass them around, but sat in the back seat and drank the lot of them. What got me about that story was that the big boss director said nothing. It was just accepted that Larry was like that. He was a character from another time, when everyone smoked in the office, had decanters of Scotch on their desks and did things in their own way. You couldn't rein Larry in, and they didn't try, because he was just too good.

Larry Fitzgerald

As well as treating the offenders with respect, my main responsibility was to accommodate the media, pure and simple. It would always amaze me when people said, 'You're just a mouthpiece for the prison system.' No shit. That was my job. But I recognised what journalists needed, which was for me to help them by being as open as I possibly could. I wasn't constrained at all, I just told the truth, which is why reporters liked me. Even when things got dicey – if there was a hostage situation, an escape or a riot – I'd always think, 'What does the media want at this point? What do I need to do to bring them into the picture?'

We had an incident in a little town called Dilley, which is south of San Antonio. There was a prison riot – or a disturbance, as we liked to call it – and all the San Antonio media immediately reacted. Those early reports were just horrible. They said guards' uniforms were being stolen, prisoners were breaking into the armoury, that there was gunfire. So I had to take control of the situation. The next day, I brought television crews inside the prison, to show them the actual damage that had been done. They were amazed, they thought they were just going to do a piece to camera out front. But I gave them a tour, and it suddenly turned into a good news story for the prison system. 'Yeah, there was a disturbance, but look how efficiently we dealt with it.' Another time, there was a reporter who was convinced we were allowing inmates to smoke in one of the warehouses while they worked. In the end, I said to him, 'You know what? I'm gonna open the door so you can see for yourself.' I did the same when a rumour went round that inmates were luxuriating in air-conditioned cells. Our philosophy at TDCJ, at least when I was there, was to be out front.

If anything bad was happening inside a penitentiary, we would call the Associated Press first and the Texas State Network, which is the largest state radio network in the US, second. We would rather tell the story to the media first, even if it had warts on it, rather than have them reacting and coming to us. That's how to handle the media. That way, you're not on the defensive. Why would we hide anything? The public needed to know, and I thought it was wrong not to be honest with them. I always used to think of Richard Nixon and Watergate: the cover-up was worse than the crime. Sure, being honest means that some bad stuff is going to come out, but at least if you're upfront about it, you can have some control over the situation.

To be honest, there were more ethical reasons: we were carrying out the ultimate bureaucratic act by executing offenders, and the media was the public's eyes on the inner workings of the system. That's why I always thought it best to get the media in there, let them interview as many offenders as they could. I thought it was to everyone's benefit: the public learned about the offender and his or her life on death row, and the offender had an opportunity to influence people's opinion of him or her. And when that offender died on the gurney, there had to be media there to witness it. We tried not to turn anybody down, because the public had a right to know we were doing things properly, not just in Texas, but all over the world.

It bothered me when there were empty media seats for an execution. I thought people should have been paying more attention. The state was taking someone's life, and most people had no idea. Even in Huntsville, there were executions that went virtually unnoticed. A guy would die on the gurney and it wouldn't even make the front page of The Huntsville Item. A few months after Karla Faye, we executed a guy called Johnny Pyles. He shot a sheriff's deputy to death in Sunnyvale in 1982, although he said it was in self-defence. Pyles was on the paint crew at Ellis, and I used to stand out in the hallway and talk to him. He'd be leaning against his podium and talking about his religious conversion, and I had no doubt he was born-again, just like Karla Faye. But, unlike Karla Faye, nobody showed up for him when he was executed. That troubled me.

When they had the first execution in Texas after the moratorium, in 1982, there were hundreds of people out front, protestors burning candles and college students swilling beer, cheering and waving signs. And I recall that when Ronald Clark O'Bryan was executed in 1984, people turned up dressed up in Halloween costumes, not because it was 31 October, but because O'Bryan had murdered his son by poisoning his trick or treat candy. I thought it was great when anti-death penalty people showed up to protest, not so much when people wanted to party. But at least they cared.

Wayne Scott, TDCJ's executive director, was real media savvy and understood that if reporters couldn't see what was happening inside the penitentiary, we should see it with our own eyes, give them the information and let them do whatever they wanted with it. If we were honest in our dealings with them in other areas, then they were more likely to trust us.

The first time I met Michelle properly was at that hostage situation we had, with Ponchai Wilkerson and Howard Guidry. I watched that situation go down. At one point, Scott said to me, 'Do Ponchai and Howard know who you are?' I told him they did, and Scott said he wanted me to lure Ponchai towards the bars, I assume so they could take him out. I was prepared to do it, but Scott changed his mind, and I'm glad he did. If I had done that, I could have kissed my job goodbye, because no inmate would have had anything to do with me. Another time, Ponchai's parents came to see him, just before his execution, and he wouldn't come out of his cell. Me and Brazzil went over there to try to talk him out, so he could say goodbye, but he just wouldn't budge. Under TDCJ rules, you were supposed to give an offender three warnings before you gassed them. I can honestly tell you, I did not hear any warnings. All of a sudden, boom! There was gas everywhere, and me and The Sinister Minister were the only staff who didn't have masks. We were beating on the door, trying to get out of the place. One good thing happened that night, though: I quit smoking, because the gas damaged my lungs so bad.

I did things in that job I shouldn't have. On Thanksgiving Day 1998, I had this feeling something weird was going to happen. Sure enough, it did. Larry Todd was the duty officer that night, and he called me up and said, 'We've had an escape from the Ellis Unit.' I said, 'Really? What's his name?' Todd told me the escapee's name was Gurule. I didn't know him, so I asked what Gurule's number was. Todd said, '619.' I said, 'Jesus Christ, that's a fucking death row inmate...' I got dressed immediately and hauled myself down there.

It was so foggy that night, which didn't help with the search, and there was media everywhere. I was working with a reporter from The New York Times, and he had an editor checking in on him. I spoke to the editor on the phone, and I just couldn't make him understand the situation. I kept saying, 'I believe the man is still on our property', and the editor from New York kept saying, 'If he's still on your property, why can't you find him?' What he didn't get was that the prison was on 17,000 acres of Texas real estate. I explained that there were all these hunting camps around the prison fences, full of guys with rifles, who would have shot Gurule in a heartbeat; there were feral hogs; fire ants; there was every poisonous snake in North America.

That was me saying, 'Gurule didn't stand a chance', but also, 'Don't come to Texas...'

Seven days after his escape, Gurule's body was hooked by a couple of TDCJ employees, who were fishing in Harmon Creek, off the Trinity River. They were not expecting to land something that big. Gurule was wearing two sets of heavy underwear and had stuffed cardboard and magazines inside his clothes, so he could roll over the razor wire without being cut up. He ran about a mile, came to a bridge and jumped off, maybe because he heard traffic coming. The river was very deep and swift-moving at that point, and they think he drowned immediately, because of all the cardboard. He must only have been free for about 45 minutes. The next day, I went out in front of the Walls Unit, where a bunch of reporters were, tore up a 'wanted' poster and said, 'Gurule is no more!' God, did I catch hell for that.

Glen Castlebury, the director of the public information office, called me 'a cowboy', and I pissed off a whole bunch of death row inmates. Gurule had a lot of fans inside the penitentiary, he was a hero to them. When they heard he'd escaped, they were all inside saying, 'Keep going, man, don't stop!' I should have said 'we got the guy', rather than being all theatrical. I just got carried away. It was an exciting job, it got the adrenalin pumping. Every time the phone rang, it was like Russian Roulette, anything could be happening...

A few of the death row inmates never spoke to Larry again. Before one execution, an inmate turned his back on him. But he won most of them round, partly because of his roguish, anti-establishment streak, partly because they needed him. Larry was the man who could land them a shot. Maybe Bianca Jagger would read about them in a newspaper and take up their cause, as happened with Gary Graham. Or maybe the Pope would get wind of their plight and make a pronouncement, denouncing the death penalty.

Larry knew offenders in a way I never got to know them, because he used to walk around death row almost as if he owned the place, dropping by for visits and chewing the fat. As he was strolling the corridors, inmates would yell out, 'Hey, Mr Fitzgerald!' Or they'd call him 'the media man'. And he loved it. All the officers loved him, too, although he could never remember their names. He called all the men 'brother' and all the women 'gal', and they'd feel so special that he'd acknowledged them at all.

CHAPTER 5
THE PARTY NEVER ENDS

'[Witnessing an execution] is like going to cover a baseball game, or a basketball game, or an explosion at a chemical factory.'

Mike Graczyk, Associated Press Texas execution witness

'Strangers in the audience... dread being caught watching the utter humiliation of another human. They dread questions in the prisoner's eyes: Who are you, and why have you come? His sins, his brokenness, his fear, his helplessness, all these are laid bare before the watching eyes of strangers.'

David Von Drehle, *Among the Lowest of the Dead*

Over the three days before an inmate's execution, guards would check his cell every 10 to 15 minutes and log everything he did. It would be trivial things, like 'inmate sleeping', 'inmate reading' or 'inmate sitting on bunk', and there were other things we'd leave off, because nobody wanted to know that an inmate had spent his final hours on earth furiously masturbating. I'd edit the log and make it part of the media packet, along with the details of the inmate's crime and a printout of his last meal request.

On the day of their execution, the inmate would eat breakfast between 3.30 and 4.30 a.m., as normal, before being taken to the visitation area at about 8 a.m. He was given four hours of visits with his family and friends, having already been given eight hours over each of the previous two days. As soon as those last visits ended, the inmate was removed from the visitation area, taken back to death row and prepared for transport to Huntsville. Once ready, he was loaded into a secure van and locked in the back with armed officers, and another vehicle containing armed officers and administrators would ride in convoy. I rode in one of those convoys once and they handed me a gun. I was terrified, sitting in the back seat thinking,

'All I need is for the driver to brake fast and me to accidentally shoot the person in front.'

The convoy usually arrived at the Walls Unit at about 1 p.m., and they'd back up the van to a special entrance and unload the inmate. Larry once said, 'These guys have been locked up for so long, but they never look up at the sky.' He was right, they never did. The inmate would be brought inside, strip-searched, given a new set of clothing, fingerprinted and put in the holding cell, which is next to the death chamber and contains a metal commode and a bunk. When he was dressed, the warden, the chaplain and I would pay the inmate a visit.

The warden would clarify who was going to witness, who was due to take possession of the inmate's belongings after death and what his last meal request was. I'd then tell him which journalists were due to witness and let him know that if he didn't want to make a last statement in the chamber, he could write one and I'd distribute it to the media. The whole time we were talking to him, I'd be sizing up his demeanour, in case any reporters asked me how he seemed before he went to his death. Mostly, they were quiet, nervous and resigned to their fate. But this one guy was particularly angry that he was about to be executed. He was about my age and the only inmate who ever called me by my first name, which just isn't done in the prison system (unless, of course, you're Larry). I wasn't about to correct him, demand he call me Ms Lyons, because he was about to die. But when he said, 'Michelle, I just don't understand why this has to happen', I replied, 'Because you killed someone and there's a price to pay.'

After we left, the inmate would be back there with some officers and a table set up with coffee, fruit punch, iced tea and snacks. Or what Larry mistakenly called 'a party platter'. *Fuck* Christiane Amanpour... The inmate was allowed to make phone calls to anywhere in the continental United States, so a lot of them would spend their final hours calling family and old friends, which you can't do on death row. I don't like saying goodbye to people at parties, so how do you end a call like that? What the hell do you say to your mother or your father or a childhood friend? One time, while we were sitting in Larry's office, Graczyk got a call from the death house and it was the condemned man wanting to talk to him. The guy was named John Satterwhite, who murdered a convenience store clerk in San Antonio in 1979. Satterwhite expressed his remorse, apologised for his crime and hung up with, 'Well, I guess I'll see you in an hour...' I was told that never once did an inmate lay down on the bunk and take a nap. Why would you, when you're about to sleep forever?

At 4 p.m., the offender's last meal was delivered. An inmate named Brian Price was responsible for preparing all the last meals, and he was outstanding. Price was a former rock musician who was taught to cook in prison by a classically trained chef. He made a point of not finding out what the condemned man had done until afterwards, because he was worried he wouldn't be able to do his best work if he knew the guy was a baby killer or serial rapist. A crew came in to make a documentary about him, and Price made mac and cheese, some of the best mac and cheese I'd ever eaten – and I've eaten a lot of it. However, if an inmate requested something the kitchen didn't have, they didn't get it. If it was filet mignon and lobster an inmate wanted, he might end up with a reconstructed burger patty and a fish stick, which is why most inmates kept it simple and ordered a cheeseburger.

I remember Price once saying, 'I had a guy order butter beans – who the hell would ask for butter beans as his last meal on earth? Then it dawned on me: I'll bet that was something his momma made for him.'

One inmate, who was into voodoo and witchcraft, requested dirt, because he planned to hold some kind of ritual in the holding cell. You know what he got instead? Yoghurt, presumably because it kind of rhymed. Gerald Mitchell requested a bag of Jolly Ranchers, another inmate asked for a jar of pickles – and was given them without the jar – and Odell Barnes asked for 'justice, equality and world peace'. Chef was all out of that, but he would have whipped him up some mean enchiladas, if only he had asked.

'[Jeffrey] Dillingham had quite a last meal. He asked for one cheeseburger with cheddar, American and mozzarella cheese, no onions, large French fries, a bowl of macaroni and cheese, lasagna with two slices of garlic bread, nacho cheese, three large cinnamon rolls, five scrambled eggs and eight pints of chocolate milk. He supposedly got everything except for that much milk. I told Larry that I would have asked for exactly the same thing minus the rolls and eggs and I would have added a Dr Pepper.'

Michelle's journal, on the execution of Jeffery Dillingham, 1 November 2000

Once the inmate had eaten his last meal, it was, in the words of Odell Barnes, 'a waiting game'. The inmate waited to die, his family waited for him to be saved, the victim's family waited for justice, the reporters waited to witness. Everybody waited.

It wasn't as if there was a clock ticking loudly on the wall and a big red phone, so that the Governor could call in personally to halt proceedings, but in 2002, James Colburn did receive a stay one minute before he was due to be moved to the death chamber. However, that rarely happened. If at 6 p.m. there were no appeals pending, the waiting would stop. If there were still appeals pending, we'd sit and wait in Larry's office some more, until we received confirmation. On Billy Vickers' first visit to the death house, none of the courts would rule and we had to wait until midnight for the death warrant to expire. Another time, the courts didn't rule until 11.23 p.m. and the execution was called off, because one of our administrators was worried we wouldn't carry it out in time and would be in violation of the order. But usually at 6 p.m., the Attorney General and Governor's offices would call the warden and give him permission to proceed, the warden would inform the inmate that it was 'time to go to the next room', and Larry would round up the reporters and lead them into the Walls Unit. Once you saw those reporters filing across the street, that execution was a go, it was not going to stop for anything.

Meanwhile, the inmate, unshackled, would be escorted from the holding cell to the death chamber by a five-member tie-down team. The inmate would walk into the death chamber, which is a tiny room painted pastel green, the colour of hospital scrubs, and an officer would say, 'Please get on the gurney.' The inmate would step up via a little stool, lie down and stretch out his arms, so that they assumed a crucifix position. Each member of the tie-down team was assigned a body part, one for each limb and one whose job was to fasten straps across the inmate's body.

The tie-down team would leave, to be replaced by the IV team. The IV team were anonymous – they would enter the death chamber, establish the IV lines, and get the saline solution flowing, before disappearing behind a wall with a one-way mirror. The IV team can see into the death chamber, but nobody can see them. I've read horror stories about inmates being strapped to the gurney for hours, waiting for the courts to make a ruling, but they're just stories – in Texas, the execution begins very shortly after the IV lines are established. Once the inmate was on the gurney and the needles were in, nothing was going to save them. It wasn't the movies.

The victim's loved ones were ushered into one witness room, opposite the inmate's head, before the inmate's loved ones were ushered into the other, opposite the inmate's feet. It was carefully choreographed, so that the two sides never saw each other. But because the walls were so thin, they could hear each other far too well. They were drab little rooms with no chairs and one big window overlooking the gurney, and the families would be right up against that glass. Sometimes, they'd shrink away, because suddenly being that close to their son or brother on the gurney – or the man who killed their mother or daughter – would spook them. I think they were shocked to discover how intimate it all was. They might look uncomfortable or afraid. They'd fidget, not know where to look. How do you possibly prepare yourself for that eventuality? But there were others who stood as close as possible, looking triumphant or defiant, sometimes even deliberately bumping against the glass.

The journalists would be divided among both sides and we'd pile in behind the families, hoping we could see. Even when I became a spokesperson, I had to have a good idea of what was going on, for the official prison record and in case reporters asked me for any colour afterwards, such as if the inmate closed his eyes or looked at the victim's family. Usually, any emotion would come from the inmate's side, because while the victim's family had had a long time to process their loss and were approaching the end of the chapter, the inmate's family were watching a loved one die. For them, the grieving process was just beginning, they were just setting out on a long, hard road. But because the walls were so thin, the victim's family could hear everything. I always thought that was cruel and it troubled me: you're someone's mom watching the person who killed your child being executed, and you've got the added stress of being forced to listen to that person's mom wailing in pain, because the thing that is supposed to bring you justice and peace is the most horrendous thing ever to happen to her.

One time, I could hear a woman sobbing and pounding the glass, another time I could hear a woman yelling and kicking the wall. There were moms who pleaded, moms who prayed and moms who insisted their son was innocent. A couple of moms even fainted. No wonder some inmates told their moms not to turn up.

Once all the witnesses were in place, we could hear the big metal door close on the inmate's side, a key turn in the lock and a prison administrator would come out from the IV room and say, 'Warden, you may proceed.' The warden would say, 'Smith, do you have a last statement?' A microphone extended from the ceiling and rested right above the inmate's mouth, and he would either say a few words or not. The warden would have told them out back in the holding cell that they'd be given a minute or so, and sometimes joke, 'Don't try to filibuster.' That's why a lot of statements would end with something like, 'That's it, warden' or 'I'm done'.

If you believe everything an inmate says in his last statement, then Texas has put hundreds of innocent men to death. But I never thought I saw an innocent man executed. Chaplain Brazzil told me some inmates had confessed to him that they were guilty of the crime, only to profess their innocence on the gurney. They'd say to him, 'There's no way I'm going out there and telling them I did it.' They'd ask him to pray for their forgiveness, and then go out and tell a bunch of lies. They did it because their family believed they didn't do it, or their mother had mortgaged her home to hire an attorney. I kind of understood, it was a condemned man trying to protect his loved ones. But once you're on that gurney and those needles are in place, you're not getting off. All hope is lost. So what benefit do you get from lying?

Some inmates would use their last statement to confess to unsolved murders, including Billy Vickers, who claimed he was a hitman and took credit for the killings of more than a dozen people. Others would try to implicate or exonerate others and give their own version of what happened. Others would accuse the police of corruption and the state of murder. Then you'd check the records and discover that their fingerprints were all over the murder weapon and there were bloody footprints leading from the scene of the crime to the inmate's door.

Ricky McGinn, the sight of whose mother, dressed in her Sunday best and with her wrinkled hands pressed against the glass still makes me cry, was the only inmate reprieved by George W. Bush during his tenure as governor. When I interviewed McGinn, he gave off the vibe of somebody who would sexually assault and kill his 12-year-old stepdaughter, which is exactly what he was accused of. But he swore he wasn't guilty and insisted that DNA tests on hair and semen evidence would prove so.

McGinn was the first inmate on Texas death row to be reprieved so that such testing could take place, leading some to suspect that Bush had only allowed it to show he was a fair guy, ahead of his nomination as the Republican presidential candidate. McGinn had changed his clothes, prayed with the chaplain and even eaten his last meal – double-cheeseburger, fries and Dr Pepper – when the warden informed him his execution had been stayed. When the tests came back, they proved McGinn was guilty, but even then he protested his innocence. I don't fault McGinn for exhausting all his options. If I was on death row, I'd do the same thing.

When he was finally executed, three months after his first date with death, McGinn didn't mention his crime, his guilt or otherwise. He said goodbye to his family, told them he loved them and prayed that God take him home.

At the moment of their death, most inmates made some reference to God. As one told me, 'You have to believe there's something beyond this place in order to have the courage to get up on that gurney.' I think that's why most of them just popped right up there. They wanted to believe they were going to a better place, although I think a lot of them were afraid they were about to go to hell. I have a very strong faith, so I understood why these men would try to make peace with the God they believed in at their moment of reckoning. I'm sure there were condemned men who claimed to be born-again who weren't. But I think a lot of them were genuine, because what else did they have in their lives apart from religion? A few men died while reciting the Lord's Prayer or verses from the Bible, a couple even died while singing hymns.

Other inmates weren't so Christian. The angriest last statement I ever heard was by Cameron Todd Willingham, who was convicted of murdering his three baby girls in a house fire in Corsicana in 1991. Like McGinn, and many others, Willingham protested his innocence to the bitter end. When the warden asked if he had anything to say, he directed a tirade at his ex-wife, who was behind the glass, that included every foul word you could imagine. The warden signalled for the injection to start while Willingham was still in full flow.

'... From God's dust I came and to dust I will return, so the earth shall become my throne. I gotta go, road dog. I love you Gabby. I hope you rot in hell, bitch. I hope you fucking rot in hell, bitch. You bitch. I hope you fucking rot, cunt. That is it.'

The real last statement of Cameron Todd Willingham, 17 February 2004

Most inmates withdrew more gracefully than Willingham. A good portion of them were extremely apologetic, if not towards their victim's family – some acted as if they weren't present in the witness room – then at least to their own. Many pleaded for forgiveness.

Some were impossibly polite. I remember one inmate speaking very eloquently about why the death penalty was wrong, before finishing off by thanking the prison system for its hospitality and his last meal, as if he was checking out of a hotel. There were plenty of shouts out 'for the boys on death row'. One inmate wanted them to know that he wasn't wearing a diaper. Quite a few last statements included a bit of light relief. One said, 'Where's my stunt double when I need him?' Patrick Knight said he was going to tell a joke on the gurney, as chosen by a member of the public. His friend put an ad out on his Myspace page and he got hundreds of submissions. A reporter asked me if I was going to participate in the frivolity, and I replied, 'We take it very seriously, so knock-knock jokes are out.' Knight must have got stage fright, because instead of telling any jokes on the gurney, he got all choked up and claimed he wasn't Patrick Knight at all.

A number of inmates just seemed relieved. There was a biker I came to know named Randall Hafdahl Sr, who used to hang out in some of the same bars as me in Galveston, though we never crossed paths in the free world. I enjoyed chatting to him about places we both knew in my hometown, as you would with anyone. He had these incredibly detailed motorcycle tattoos that he'd done himself in prison. He certainly had a bit more class than Martin Robles, who had a tattoo of a demon eating the brains of Jesus Christ on one of his biceps. I took photos of Hafdahl's inkings before he died, so his attorney could send them to his daughter. In exchange, his attorney sent me photos of little wooden motorcycles that Hafdahl carved while he was on death row. Because he was a nomad, being confined was a living hell and he was absolutely ready to go.

There's a singer from Houston named Robert Earl Keen, and his signature song is 'The Road Goes on Forever'. It's about a man who kills a cop and is sentenced to death, which is exactly what happened to Hafdahl, who gunned down a police officer in Amarillo in 1985 before being executed 17 years later. Hafdahl quoted that song on the gurney, 'The road goes on forever and the party never ends! Let's rock and roll!' For years he'd been locked up in this tiny room, like a bird in a cage. Now he was dead, but so happy to finally be free.

> '... I've been hanging around this popsicle stand way too long. Before I leave, I want to tell you all, when I die, bury me deep, lay two speakers at my feet, put some headphones on my head and rock and roll me when I'm dead. I'll see you in heaven some day. That's all, Warden.'
>
> **Last statement of Douglas Roberts, 20 April 2005**

Perhaps the most nonsensical last statement I ever heard was by Monty Delk, who shot a man to death in Crockett in 1986 and was one of death row's most notorious inmates. He refused to shower, smeared himself with his own faeces and had to be segregated from other inmates because he smelled so bad. Delk also claimed to be 129 years old, a former submarine commander, a former president of Kenya, and to have been killed 150 times in prison. However, prison psychiatrists claimed he was pretending to be insane to avoid the death penalty. I really couldn't tell with some inmates. Johnny Penry was convicted of a rape and murder but got off death row because the courts decided he was intellectually retarded. They said he couldn't read or write, but he said to me once, 'Did you read the story about me in *Talk* magazine? That was a damn good article.' I said, 'You read it?' He caught himself and said, 'No, I got somebody to read it to me.'

Before Delk was executed in 2002, he refused to take a shower, so the officers tried to bribe him with a Coke. He took the Coke, but his shower consisted of him simply standing under the water without scrubbing, which didn't help the stench as much as had been hoped. His last words were, 'You are not in America. This is the island of Barbados. People will see you doing this.' To me, that sounded a lot like somebody doing their best impersonation of a madman. After he had finished speaking, his eyes shot open, as sometimes happened when the drugs started flowing.

In contrast, there were last statements that were profound in their simplicity, the shorter the sweeter. David Martinez, who raped and murdered a student in Austin in 1997 before being executed in 2005, went out with, 'Only the sky and the green grass goes on forever and today is a good day to die.' That was that. Other inmates just seemed slightly befuddled. They'd ask the warden if the microphone was on, who was standing behind the glass or sound slightly apologetic because they didn't have anything to say. James Clark, who was executed in 2007, only realised anyone had shown up to witness at the very last moment, when he happened to look to his right. His last word, on seeing some faces peering back at him from the witness rooms, was an incongruous 'howdy'.

I never saw an inmate pleading for his life, and I can only recall one man outright sobbing on the gurney, which will probably amaze a lot of people. Most of the sobbing had been done a long time ago, just as most of the anger had evaporated. It was about trying to take it like a man. Of course, there were plenty of inmates who said nothing at all. The warden would ask if they had a last statement and they would shake their head. The next noise you'd hear was their last breath, which was their lungs collapsing and pushing the air out, like a set of bellows.

It used to be that the warden had a signal – when he took his glasses off, the IV team would know to start the flow of drugs. But somehow word got out, and one day an inmate kept asking the warden, 'Is this when you take your glasses off?' So they came up with a new method, a little controller, like a garage door opener, and when the warden pressed the button, a light went on in the IV room.

All the executions I saw were carried out using the three-drug method. The first drug, sodium thiopental, was a sedative administered in a lethal dose, significant enough to kill you even without the other two. After it was administered, inmates would become groggy, their eyes would start closing and they'd sometimes say they could taste it, and that it tasted bad. I never saw anybody say anything about feeling pain, which eventually made me think: if that were me being executed, I would try to remember to scream or start shouting about how much it hurt, because even if it didn't halt my execution, it might at least trigger a moratorium on the death penalty. And how would anyone be able to prove that I had been lying? Apparently, one time, an inmate's vein did blow and the IV line shot off and started spraying the walls with saline. I never saw any issues with the IV lines, although one guy, who had been a prolific drug user, had to have a needle in his neck, because they couldn't find another usable vein. Because of the proximity to the microphone, we could hear the chemicals gurgling as they entered his body.

The second drug, pancuronium bromide, is a muscle relaxant, also administered in a lethal dose, designed to collapse the lungs and diaphragm. The noise was always different, often depending on whether they fought it or not. Anybody's instinct is to fight and gulp for air, like a fish on dry land, but Chaplain Brazzil used to tell them to think of it as a wave, and not to fight the wave, but go with it. That way, Brazzil told them, it would be an easier transition. That last breath might sound like a cough, a gasp, a snore, a rattle, a whimper or the snorting of a horse. The third drug, potassium chloride, stopped the heart. But by the time that third drug was flowing, silence had already descended.

'I thought it was going to be harder than this...'

Last statement of Rogelio Cannady, 19 May 2010

That silence lasted five or six minutes. The warden would remain by the inmate's head, and Chaplain Brazzil would still have his hand on the inmate's knee. Sometimes, Brazzil would catch my eye and give me a wink, as if to say, 'Sorry, but it's gonna be okay.' He was such a sweet, kind-hearted man. I'd stand stiff behind the glass, stomach grumbling, that strange smell in my nostrils, watching the inmate turn purple.

For the longest time when I was a reporter, I'd seen Graczyk leaning forward and looking at something on the ceiling, but couldn't work out what it was. Eventually, I realised there was a red light up there, which remained on while the chemicals were being administered and went off when the process was finished. Minutes later, the warden would fetch the doctor, the doctor would enter the chamber, check for a heartbeat with his stethoscope and announce the official time of death, which was always five or six minutes later than the actual time of death. Then the warden would lean into the microphone and repeat, for the benefit of his secretary, who was transcribing the official account of the night's events from an office. Brazzil would put his hand over the inmate's face and, if they were open, close their eyes. I assume he was saying a little prayer. Then he'd pull the sheet over their face and we'd be free to leave.

Having worked as a police reporter while still at college, I joined my father at *The Huntsville Item* in 1998. I had always been interested in crime – and crime doesn't come any bigger or crazier than in Texas.

Since 1924, every execution in Texas has taken place in Huntsville, in the Walls Unit's death chamber. Between 1924 and 1964, 361 offenders were executed by electric chair. Since 1982, lethal injection has been the preferred method.

Ex 10-1-98

Name: Javier Cruz

D.R. # 999061

DOB: 9 / 13 / 57   **Received:** 4 / 30 / 93   **Age:** 35   (when rec'd)

County: Bexar

Date of offense: 6 / 7 / 91
7 14 91

Age at time of offense: 33   **Race:** Hispanic   **Height:** 5-7

Weight: 208   **Eyes:** brown   **Hair:** black

Native County: Webb   **State:** Texas

Prior Occupation: feed store clerk   **Education level:** 9 years

Prior prison record:

TDCJ #387174, rec. 11/16/84 from Bexar Co., 5 years, poss. of heroin, paroled under mandatory supervision to Bexar Co. 4/24/85, returned as MS violator w/o new charges 12/18/87, paroled under MS 3/18/88, returned as MS violator w/o new charges 1/10/92, bench warrant to Bexar Co. 3/9/92 returned with death sentence.

Summary: Convicted in the strangulation murders of Louis Menard Neal, 71, and James Michael Ryan, 69, at the victim's homes in San Antonio. Neal was gagged and his hands bound behind his back with a sock before he was beaten with a hammer and strangled with a bathrobe belt. His decomposing body was found hanging by the neck from a towel rod inside his North Alamo Street apartment five days after the June 7, 1991 murder. Ryan's nude body was found inside his Mandalay Street residence the day after his July 14, 1991 murder. He also had been strangled and his television and automobile stolen. Cruz's accomplice later told police that they sold the tires off of Ryan's Cadillac to buy heroin. Cruz was arrested in the murders on Oct. 22, 1991.

Co-Defendants:

Antonio Omero Ovalle, H/M, DOB: 6/25/61, Rec. 2/3/93 #633446. Agreed to testify against Cruz and plead guilty to murder, agg. robbery and attempted burglary in exchange for two consecutive life sentences.

Race of Victim(s):

One black male (Neal) & one white male (Ryan)

The first inmate I saw executed was Javier Cruz, on 2 October 1998. It was my role as a reporter to document the procedure, and watching Cruz die left me unmoved. I was 22 years old and supported the death penalty.

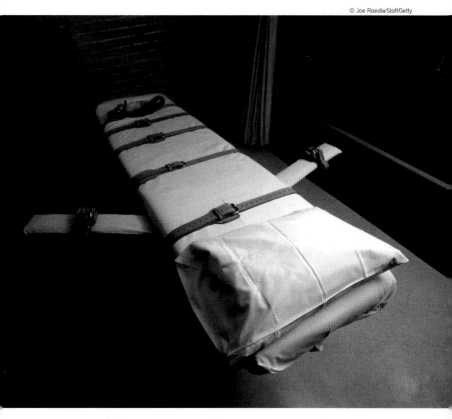

The death chamber is a tiny room containing little more than a gurney. To the right of the inmate's head are witness rooms, where loved ones of inmates and victims, plus reporters and prison staff, watch the execution. I know that room well.

Send unique, personal greetings with *Happy Horse* cards by Billy Hughes, Jr.

Inmates can spend decades on death row. Billy Hughes Jr., the first condemned man I interviewed for the *Item*, stayed busy during his 24-year stay, earning college degrees, translating books into braille and running a greetings card business.

www.deathrow.at/freebob/

Michelle Lyons
TDCJ Media Relations
P.O. BOX 99
Huntsville, TX 77342

Ms. Lyons,

Hi, if you are reading this then they killed me. I just wanted to tell you
that I enjoyed talking to you, you seem like a really great lady. I'm sorry
we didn't meet under different circumstances, I would have liked to have gotten
to know you better. I hope when you think of me you will smile and have good
thoughts. I wish you all the luck in the world. Take care. Give yourself
a hug for me. Thank you for your kindness. Have a wonderful day.

Best wishes,

Bob Coulson

P.S.: DON'T LET ANYONE STEAL YOUR SMILE!!!

Robert Coulson was sentenced to death for the murder of five members
of his own family, as well as an unborn baby. A few days before reading
this rather sweet letter, I had watched him die on the gurney.

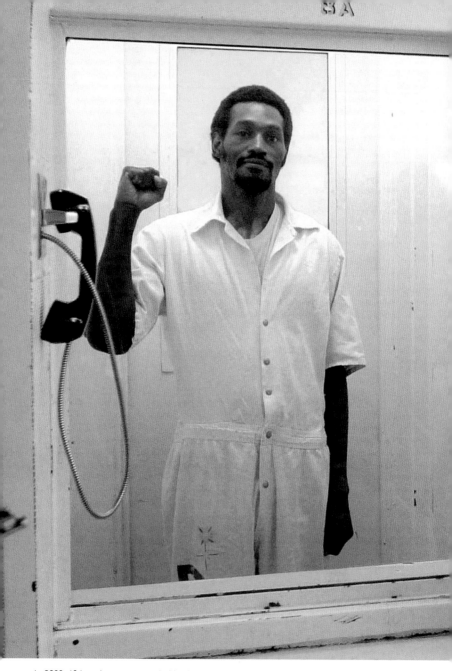

In 2000, 40 inmates were executed in Huntsville, a record for the most executions in a single year by an individual state. Of the 38 I witnessed that year, the most dramatic was that of anti-death penalty poster boy, Gary Graham.

7A

Gary Graham's execution was witnessed by the Reverends Jesse Jackson and Al Sharpton, and Bianca Jagger. The New Black Panthers, toting AK47s, and the Ku Klux Klan also turned up. It was like a fucking zoo.

During George W. Bush's governorship, 152 executions took place in Texas. But because the death penalty was popular in the state, demonstrations such as at Graham's execution were rare.

CHAPTER 6
A STRANGE KIND OF FELLOW

'For us, what the Americans are doing is completely incomprehensible, that such an advanced country can be involved in such an act of barbarism.'

Henri Leclerc, former president of the Human Rights League

'The girls were still being raped when Cantu whispered to Venancio, "We're going to have to kill them." When everyone was finished, Cantu told them to take the girls into the woods, where they proceeded to strangle them. Cantu kicked Elizabeth in the face with his steel toe boots, knocking out several teeth, and he stepped on Jennifer's neck until she stopped moving. Subsequently, they all took turns stomping on both girls' necks to make sure they were dead.'

Texas Attorney General media advisory on Peter Cantu, sentenced to death for the murders of Elizabeth Peña and Jennifer Ertman in 1994

I had friends who loved telling people what I did for a living. We'd be in a bar, I'd see the excitement on their face and know exactly what they were about to say: 'Tell them what you do!' It always felt weird talking about it with anyone new. I was aware I had an interesting job, a different job, and I knew people would be fascinated and want to ask questions. But I didn't want to sound too forthcoming: 'Oh yeah, I watch people die. What else would you like to know?' Some people were repulsed by it, particularly one girl I'd gone to school with. The fact she felt like that really pissed me off. I thought, 'You don't really have any idea. You don't know what I feel about it inside. You're repulsed because I go into that room? But that's my job, and it's an important job, so how dare you judge me?'

I met my first husband in 2002. He was raised in Huntsville and went to Texas A&M, although I didn't know him then. When I met him, at an A&M memorial event in Huntsville, I thought he was a good-looking man, and I liked the fact he seemed so quiet and serious. I'm not serious, at least on the outside, I joke around and say crazy things. But I thought, 'I'm gonna shake this guy up.'

Having grown up in Galveston, I was all rap music and flip-flops, whereas he was more cowboy boots and country music. But we hit it off, that opposites attract cliché was true in our case.

Being from Huntsville, he knew lots of people who worked for the prison system, so my job didn't bother him, he didn't find it weird. He thought it was interesting, like everybody thought it was interesting, but we didn't talk about it a ton. He did ask, but I'd tell him everything was fine and change the subject. When I clocked off, I tried to leave the job behind, I didn't want it in my home. Then again, I didn't really think about it in those terms at the time, because I still didn't think it was taking a toll on me.

George W. Bush became president in January 2001 and was replaced as Texas Governor by Rick Perry. Perry's first year in charge saw a drop-off in executions – 17 offenders were put to death in 2001 – but the chamber got busy again in 2002, with 33 men dying on the gurney. But I can't stress enough that witnessing executions was only a small part of the job. As well as administrative issues, which was the vast majority of what I dealt with, there were death row media days every Wednesday, which meant spending time with the inmates, which was often a fascinating experience.

People in America are disgusted by the amount of crime in their country, but intrigued by it at the same time. I watched true crime shows all the time, especially the Investigation Discovery Channel, because I wanted to know what made criminals do the despicable things they did. Here's a riddle: At her grandmother's funeral, a woman makes eye contact with a man across the room. She's suddenly filled with a feeling she's never had before, that this is the man for her. They keep staring at each other and are both overcome by emotion. The funeral ends, everybody breaks up and she loses sight of him. He's left and gone home. Later that night, she goes home and murders her sister. Why?

If you answered correctly, the FBI think you might be a sociopath. Here it is: If the man knew her grandmother well enough to go to her funeral, he'd probably come to her sister's funeral as well, which meant she would get the chance to see him again, and this time speak to him. I had two family members who got it right.

That kind of stuff fascinates me. It's because sociopaths lack the ability to empathise that they are able to do these seemingly crazy things. Like breaking into a stranger's home, hiding in their closet and murdering them, because your girlfriend wants to leave you. Or dangling a doll over your stepdaughter's crib, in a hangman's noose, like Daniel Hittle, who also killed his adoptive parents because their dog scratched his truck. Or killing a woman, defiling her dead body and dousing her decomposing corpse with perfume, so you can defile her dead body some more, like Jose Santellan did in a Fredericksburg motel room in 1993. When he confessed, he said he wanted to lie in bed with her, to show how much he loved her. I'll never forget the prosecutor's comment: 'Santellan is a strange kind of fellow...' On death row, I got to see these kinds of people up close.

I would sometimes sit and listen to an inmate's interview, and after the interview was done and they were waiting to be taken back to their cell, I'd have a chat with them. If they wanted to talk for a while, I didn't see any reason not to. They'd all done horrible things, but there was no need to be shitty to them. I quickly discovered that the vast majority weren't the monsters I thought they might be, although there were a few who showed glimpses of their disturbed mental condition and manipulative powers.

There was Tommy Sells, who had killed the Dardeen family in Benton, Illinois, a crime that still plagued the community years after it happened. I'd interviewed him for the *Item*, and because he was convicted of a terrible crime in Del Rio, Texas, when a little girl had her throat slit while she was having a sleepover with a friend, and claimed to have killed dozens more, I got to know him pretty well in my capacity as a prison spokesperson, because a lot of reporters wanted to grill him.

Sells was such an ass: very rude, smug and disrespectful. One time, he was trying to justify everything he'd done by claiming he only killed when he felt threatened, so I said, 'How did that two-year-old make you feel threatened?' He started sobbing. Reporters used to be able to buy inmates drinks and snacks from a vending machine, but we had to do away with that, because people like Sells started threatening to pull the plug on interviews if they didn't get the treats they wanted. I remember Sells throwing a tantrum because he wanted a Mountain Dew, and I finally lost it. 'You know you need to knock that shit off, because I don't care if you do the interview or not.'

Another guy I didn't get along with was Cesar Fierro. Fierro was a Mexican national who had been on death row since 1980 for murdering a cab driver in El Paso. Because some people thought Fierro was innocent, and he'd been stayed so many times, he had plenty of visits, and his interviews were sometimes conducted in Spanish. One time, he was signing his media release form and said in Spanish to the reporter, 'I like this pen.' The reporter replied, 'Oh, in that case it's yours...' Fierro didn't realise I understood Spanish. That pen belonged to a correctional officer, and Fierro could have killed somebody with it. I jumped in, told Fierro he couldn't have it, and he went absolutely apeshit. He was screaming, calling me a whore, and spitting and banging on the glass. So I did something that was kind of mean. I made sure that nobody else could see me, stepped forward, smiled real big and mouthed: 'Fuck off...' He got even madder, if that was possible. I was shrugging my shoulders and saying to the officers, 'Why is he doing that? I don't know what's wrong with him...' Fierro remains on death row, where he has been mouldering for almost 38 years.

Larry Fitzgerald

I took my wife Marianne to death row once. She saw Ponchai Wilkerson and said, 'Who's that nice-looking black guy with the great body?' I said, 'He's a murderer.' I introduced her to some of the offenders

I had relationships with and when we came to Kenneth McDuff's cell, he got up off his bunk and stuck out his hand for Marianne to shake it. She didn't. I had friends on death row, but alongside them were people I considered to be truly evil, and Kenneth Allen McDuff was one of them. McDuff was one of the worst people you'd ever want to meet.

In 1966, McDuff was sentenced to die in the electric chair for the kidnapping and brutal murder of three teenagers in Everman. The girl was raped for hours, before having her neck snapped with a broomstick, hence his nickname, 'The Broomstick Killer'. According to his accomplice, McDuff told his victim, 'We're gonna wear you out.' When the Supreme Court struck the death penalty in 1972, and having already received a couple of stays of execution, McDuff's sentence was commuted to life in prison. After he was released into the general population, McDuff became a boss. He had his own 'punk', who provided him with drugs and sexual favours in exchange for protection from some white supremacists his punk had managed to piss off. Among his other transgressions, McDuff was convicted of attempting to bribe a parole board member.

But McDuff was rare among inmates in that he was from a middle-class background, and his parents were able to hire an expensive lawyer, who pinned the murders on McDuff's accomplice. In 1989, partly because of the efforts of his lawyer, and partly because Texas' prisons were bulging at the seams and running out of beds, McDuff made parole, to the dismay of pretty much anybody with half a brain.

Over the next few years, McDuff murdered at least four more women in the Waco area and another in Austin. He was finally arrested in Kansas City, Missouri, after a massive manhunt and an appearance on America's Most Wanted. McDuff has the dubious honour of being the only man in Texas history to be sent to death row and paroled, before being sent back to death row again. McDuff's initial release and recidivism also led directly to a complete overhaul of the Texas parole system, in the form of statutes known as the McDuff Laws, and the building of billions of dollars' worth of new prisons. McDuff made quite a splash.

When McDuff was at the Ellis Unit, I got closer to him than probably anyone. I'd read up on him, and knew he was a momma's boy. I'd go by his cell and he'd be stretched out on his cot. He was generally withdrawn, but as soon as I mentioned his mom, he'd get up and talk to me. I'd say to him, 'Have you talked to Addie lately?' and McDuff would suddenly become quite animated. But he never asked me my name, and I never felt comfortable enough to go into his cell.

To my knowledge, I only ever saw one inmate executed who had been convicted as a serial killer – as defined as a person who kills three or more people – and that was Daniel Corwin, who murdered three women in 1987, two of them in Huntsville. He abducted one at a car wash and stabbed her to death while her three-year-old daughter was watching from inside the vehicle. McDuff was only convicted of murdering two people second time around – Melissa Northrup and Colleen Reed – but they think he did as many as 16. He was cordial *with me, and didn't act up on death row. But he was also the biggest monster I met, a picture-perfect psychopath.*

McDuff generally refused media interviews, but there was this female reporter who worked for the NBC station out of Austin who managed to speak to him four or five times. She was this attractive little brunette lady, and finally I said to her one day, 'You know why McDuff likes you to interview him?' She said, 'No. Why?' And I said, 'Because you look like his victims.' She stopped interviewing him after that.

On the afternoon of his execution, I went back there and they were fingerprinting him, which always amazed me: you've got to fingerprint the offender minutes before he's going to be executed, to make sure you've got the right man? When they strip-searched him, I noticed that his testicles were greatly enlarged. He was standing buck-assed naked in front of me, so I could hardly miss them, they looked like goddamn baseballs. So I said, 'Jesus, McDuff, what's wrong with you?' He said it was because of all the alcohol he'd been drinking, and I said, 'Damn, McDuff, you haven't been out on the street for years, how can you have been drinking that much liquor?' He kind of laughed and replied, 'You never heard of "chalk"?' 'Chalk' is prison slang for home-made booze.

As I was leaving, he said, 'Hey, media man, I wanna know one thing – did I draw a bigger crowd than Karla Faye?' I replied, 'No, McDuff, you did not...' Because he'd managed to slither through the cracks for so long, I got the impression he didn't think he was going to be executed, so was totally unprepared. But something happened between the holding cell and the death chamber, because his final words were, 'I'm ready to be released.' When he was pronounced dead, me and one of the US Marshals who arrested him did a high-five in the witness room, which was the only time that happened.

Brazzil asked me to attend McDuff's funeral, which took place in the prison graveyard, where some of Texas' more famous outlaws are buried. The Joe Byrd Cemetery, colloquially known as Peckerwood Hill, is on a beautiful plot of land and laid out like Arlington, with neat rows of crosses. It's really a tranquil place, but also sad. They're essentially paupers' graves, for prisoners who died in the system and weren't claimed by their families. Most of the more recent headstones have the inmate's name, but McDuff has a simple stone cross with his date of death, an 'X' for executed and his prison number, which I'll never forget: 999055. At McDuff's burial, there was a young male and female there, who made a statement: 'You don't know how difficult it is to be named McDuff in this state. We're glad to see him dead.' I wasn't surprised, because even Brazzil had trouble digesting the crimes of some of the inmates he ministered to...

'After McDuff had put his underwear back on, they took a picture of him. He wasn't bad-looking in his youth, but standing there in that cell in his underwear, he was a broken old man. He had no pride, no anger, had thrown it all away.

'I wasn't for the death penalty or against the death penalty, and I didn't want to watch those people die. But I needed to give them the best comfort I could. I treated a condemned man the same as I did a little girl dying of cancer in hospital.

'It made me appreciate life, but it took its toll. After an execution, I'd go home and cry. It made me angry at people. Trying to keep myself spiritually strong was a day-to-day struggle. Those three hours I spent with an inmate on the day of his execution were real. When you're talking to a man that has three hours to live and is 13 steps from the gurney, he's not playing games with you. It got really nitty-gritty.

'I was in the death chamber with 155 inmates, and I got many of them to sign my Bible. But there was one inmate who had done a horrendous crime, and I couldn't see past it, because I was so angry. As I was trying to talk to him about God, the words were just dribbling out. I told him, "I need to talk to the warden outside." After about 30 minutes, I realised that I was looking at the inmate through my own eyes, and not God's. It wasn't about me, it was about the inmate and his needs. The warden said, "You haven't done anything we haven't all done. Now go back in and do your job."'

Jim Brazzil, former Huntsville Unit chaplain

I never really felt unsafe, although inmates liked to play games. One time, I was talking to a guy and he said, 'I read your dad's column in *The Huntsville Item*, about you and your brother...' There was no specific threat, but that was him saying he knew things about me, to make me uncomfortable. Death row officers learned not to park on one particular side of the building, because inmates used to stand on their bunks, look out of their little windows and see which officers drove which cars. The next time they saw them, they'd say, 'Hey, how you liking that black truck?' Prison inmates are divested of their power, so that was an easy win for them, a semblance of control.

There were only a couple of occasions I looked into an inmate's eyes and thought I saw pure evil. Douglas Feldman was a university graduate and former financial analyst who was riding his motorcycle one night in Dallas, snapped and started shooting at truck drivers. He killed two in one night, before wounding another victim a week later. While in prison, he was a serial troublemaker, and once ripped a phone from the wall before a scheduled media interview. He didn't get any visits after that. What really pissed off the correctional officers and his fellow death row inmates was the fact he had this creepy whistle and wouldn't shut up. The irony was, he said unnecessary noise made him violent. But for me it was his eyes.

While on death row, Feldman wrote letters, in which he compared killing humans to hunting animals. In one, he said: 'I have come to hate every single person on this planet with all my heart and soul. If I had a button which would kill every single person, I would push it with no hesitation whatsoever.' And that's what looking at him was like, as if he was a hunter and I was his prey.

Ángel Reséndiz was a rare Hispanic serial killer – serial killers tend to be white men – who was linked to a whole bunch of murders across America and Mexico. The media nicknamed him 'The Railroad Killer', because he criss-crossed the country by freight train, and he was sentenced to death for the 1998 killing of a doctor, who lived by some railway tracks in Houston. Claudia Benton was raped, stabbed with a kitchen knife and bludgeoned with a bronze statue, eight days before Christmas.

Reséndiz claimed he was half-man, half-angel and therefore couldn't die. He was one of the strangest people I ever met, and also one of the scariest. I'd always be very honest and open with most of these men, no different to if I'd just met them in a bar, so they'd speak quite freely. The people he killed were so varied, which was unusual for a serial killer. He told me he killed Claudia Benton because when he broke into her house, she had pictures of foetuses, and he reasoned that she must support abortion, was evil and must die (Benton was actually a paediatric geneticist, specialising in childhood diseases). He said he killed a young couple because when he broke into their house, he saw a picture of the man in military uniform, assumed they must support war and therefore must die. He once told me he'd killed about 40 people, and he was just so matter-of-fact about it. I asked him, 'Aren't you evil, if you're killing all these people?' And he answered, 'No, because I'm eradicating the world of evil.' So I said, 'If you broke into my house and saw something you thought made me evil, I would have to die?' He smiled and said, 'Yes.'

Reséndiz might have said he was half-man, half-angel, but he was actually very smart. In summer, he'd miraculously become a 'cutter' (an inmate who habitually cuts himself), because the only prison units in Texas that were air-conditioned were the medical and psychiatric units. On death row, inmates baked in their cells for 23 or 24 hours a day, and it's amazing how well-behaved Reséndiz was in the winter months. He was cooperative with the media and knew exactly what they wanted from him. You'd see him telling reporters how to set up the mic clips on the phone, and he'd pose for pictures with his hands against the glass.

Reséndiz was also extremely creepy. When a reporter gave him a Coke – it had to be Coke, not Pepsi – he would insist on posing with it and ask them to take a picture. I'd be thinking, 'Does he think he's gonna get a commercial deal or something? "Coca-Cola – the preferred drink of death row inmates". It's not gonna happen, Reséndiz!' He was also selling his finger- and toenail clippings on eBay. The really gross part was that people were buying them – there are actually people out there who will spend $200 on a bag of a serial killer's fingernails! There was a guy who worked in the Houston mayor's office who was a crusader against what they call 'murderbilia', so he contacted me, let me know about this creepy side business, and we put a stop to it. Santa Claus presumably let a few people down that Christmas.

Reséndiz would also flirt with me, told me he liked it when I wore red, so I never wore red again. One time, a reporter was buying him a snack, I asked Reséndiz what he wanted and he replied, 'Anything that looks as good as you.' I said, 'Ewwww! You know what? You're getting doughnuts...' When I hung up the phone, he was laughing on the other side of the glass. You could have offered me a million dollars to be in a room with him and I would have refused, because I felt he would have killed me for sure.

> 'I spoke briefly with Reséndiz before his interview. He told me I look more beautiful every time he sees me. Thanks, serial killer...'
>
> **Michelle, death row media notes, 20 February 2002**

I got why inmates would want to talk to a woman, because they didn't get to see many on death row. There was one inmate who didn't speak English, and spoke Spanish with lots of slang, so that I didn't really understand what he was saying to me. For all I know, he was saying he planned to find out where my family lived and have them all killed, while I was smiling and nodding. He became somewhat enamoured of me and kept making necklaces and sending them to my office. One was a crucifix, with a little string Jesus; another was a heart with my initial on it. I soon stopped talking to him. But while there was a bit of borderline flirtation from some of the men, inmates were rarely inappropriate. Most of the time we'd just chat nonsense.

One inmate, this young, very good-looking Hispanic man, admitted to his crime, and I said, 'Oh, so you did it?' And he laughed and said, 'Yeah, we can't all be innocent!' He was funny as hell. Another inmate said, albeit with a huge smile on his face, 'I heard you're mean.' Apparently, someone had seen me kick out a German TV crew for not obeying the rules. The cameraman kept filming inmates without permission, I gave him three warnings and he wouldn't listen, so I had an officer pull the microphone off the inmate he was supposed to be filming and told them to leave. As Fitzgerald always used to say, 'These European journalists all understand English until you tell them "no".' The reporter was almost in tears and the rumour spread that I was some kind of badass who made people cry. The inmates were like old women, gossiping over the fence.

Another inmate had heard I was a goth. I did have black hair and wear dark lipstick, and you weren't allowed to wear white in the prison system, in case something went off and you got confused with the prisoners, but I never set out to be a goth like Robert Smith of The Cure! That cracked me up.

Rodolfo Hernandez was trafficking five illegal Mexican immigrants in 1985 when he robbed and shot them all, killing one of them. While he was on death row, he contracted diabetes and one of his legs was amputated. When he requested a prosthetic, because he wanted to walk to his death, 'like a man', the prison system scoffed at the idea, saying he didn't need one and that it would cost too much money. So Larry and I leaked the story to the media. It just seemed like the right thing to do, and we didn't understand why the prison system was being so unreasonable about it.

Should we have shown sympathy for his plight? Probably not, this man was a murderer. But it was the older inmates, those who had been on death row for years, I usually felt sorry for. Maybe it was because the person I saw, all grey and weathered, was so different to the person I'd seen in the mugshots. They were no longer that young, dumb kid who committed the crime. Or maybe my empathy for Hernandez was a sign that that mental suitcase was beginning to get full.

The day before Hernandez was scheduled to be executed, he had some media interviews set up, and the police also came along, because they knew he had details about some unsolved murders. It was the rule that lawyers weren't allowed to be present during interviews, but Hernandez's lawyer refused to leave the room, because she didn't want him to admit to anything. Presumably she thought it would make it harder for her to get him off at the last moment. I told her she needed to leave, she and I got into it, and finally she flounced out. As she was leaving, she said to Hernandez, 'You don't say one thing!' The minute she was out of the door, Hernandez said he wanted to talk to the police. He spent a long time telling them about all these other murders he'd committed as a hitman and they stayed his execution, so that he could clear up all these cases. Afterwards, he thanked me for kicking his lawyer out, because he'd been able to get those things off his conscience.

Hernandez had been really nervous before his first execution date, to the extent that he wasn't able to eat. But when it was time for his second, he was a totally different person. He was suddenly so calm and ready, because he had nothing weighing him down any more. I said to him, 'Oh, I see you're eating this time?' And he replied, 'Yeah, because I know I did the right thing.' He never did get his prosthetic leg. The media leak worked, and the prison system did try, but they couldn't fit him for one because he had a serious staph infection.

On the day of Hernandez's execution, I was speaking to him in Spanish when he told me I reminded him of his daughter. Then he offered me his hand, and I froze. A year earlier, an inmate named Juan Soria had been visited by a 78-year-old chaplain on death row. When Soria asked the chaplain to pray with him, the chaplain put his hand through the food tray slot and Soria yanked him in, breaking his arm in the process. Soria then tied a sheet around the chaplain's wrist – the other end was attached to his bed – and attempted to cut his arm off with two razor blades. The ordeal went on for so long, correctional officers eventually had to gas Soria to free the chaplain. When Hernandez put his hand out, I was surrounded by officers and thinking, 'God, they're going to judge me whatever I do...' After a couple of seconds, I stuck my hand a few inches inside the bars of his holding cell and he shook it. Or at least he shook my fingertips. He was the only inmate I ever touched. I was worried that somebody might think bad of me, but a tad more worried about his infection. I spent the rest of the day scrubbing those fingertips for dear life.

'He looked up, his voice was full of emotion and I think his eyes had tears in them. He said, "Y'all are going to kill me tonight." I looked at him and said, "This is the part of my job I hate the most. I just work in the media office... I don't enjoy this... I can't imagine what you must be feeling..." He was looking at me like, "Why are you leaving?" But it was time for me to go...'

Michelle's notes on the execution of Daniel Earl Reneau, 13 June 2002

CHAPTER 7
LOOK AGAIN

'Napoleon Beazley's government is planning to kill him on 15 August 2001 for a murder committed when he was aged 17. If he lived in China, or Yemen, or Kyrgyzstan, or Kenya, or Russia, or Indonesia, or Japan, or Cuba, or Singapore, or Guatemala, or Cameroon, or Syria, or almost any other of the diminishing number of countries that retain the death penalty, Napoleon Beazley would not be confronting this fate. But he lives, and is scheduled to die, in the United States of America.'

Amnesty International

'Words seem trite in describing what follows when your husband is murdered in your presence, when your father is stripped from your life. The horror, the agony, the emptiness, the despair, the chaos, the confusion. The sense that one's life no longer has any purpose... Crimes such as those committed against my family are intolerable in any society that calls itself not only free, but civilised.'

J. Michael Luttig, son of Napoleon Beazley murder victim John Luttig

Napoleon Beazley made that hole in one, receiving a last-minute stay of execution from the Texas Court of Criminal Appeals. But in April 2002, after seven years on death row, his stay was lifted and his execution rescheduled for the following month. In the months since I'd interviewed him for *The Huntsville Item*, I'd met him a ton of times, because he was the poster child for juvenile executions and so many media outlets wanted to do stories on him. Working for the prison system, I got to go behind the curtain, and I now saw Napoleon in a different light. Because we were from similar backgrounds and about the same age, we had a good rapport. He was a funny guy, would tell little jokes. One time, he asked me what I did, I told him and he said, 'You watch executions? That's some sick shit!' I wrote it down because I thought it was so funny.

There were other inmates who seemed like they were genuinely sorry for their crime, and most people on death row didn't set out to do what they did. They weren't true psychopaths, in that they didn't wake up one morning and decide to kill someone. Maybe they set out to burglarise a house or rob someone and it ended up in murder. But Napoleon was on a different level altogether. Not only did I get the sense that he wouldn't have been in any more trouble, I thought he would have been a productive member of society, were he given a second chance. He could have done great things. When someone is found guilty of capital murder, a question a jury is supposed to answer is, 'Is this person a future danger?' In Napoleon's case, I think the jury got it wrong. Then again, you never thought Napoleon would have done what he did in the first place, so I can understand why jurors thought like they did.

It seemed like everyone who came into contact with Napoleon liked him. His fellow death row inmates liked him, the correctional officers liked him, the reporters liked him. They all knew he was guilty of the crime, but I think a lot of them were rooting for him to get another stay or for his sentence to be commuted. Jeffery Doughtie, who occupied the cell next door, told me how bad he felt about his neighbour's impending death: 'Napoleon hadn't even learned how to live, and he's having to learn how to die.' I was rooting for him, too, but felt guilty about feeling that way. That's what made Napoleon's case so complicated. It was easy for me to say Napoleon had fallen in with a bad crowd, had done a stupid thing and, if given another chance, wouldn't have done anything like it again. He didn't kill my dad while my mom was lying on the floor, pretending to be dead. It was a heinous crime. His victims were in their home, where they thought they'd be safe. Had I been J. Michael Luttig, I'd have absolutely wanted Napoleon to be executed. Did I have any right to feel sympathy, when Napoleon didn't take anything from me?

On the morning of 28 May 2002, Larry and I visited Napoleon in the holding cell. We met him at 1.24 p.m., and I wrote on my notepad: 'Smaller than I thought.' I had no idea he was that short, because this was the first time I'd seen him standing up. Whenever I'd seen him in the visitation area on death row, he'd been sitting down, in a booth behind the Plexiglass. He was quite well built, a football player, so in my mind he was this tall guy. Suddenly, Napoleon wasn't the same person. As well as shrinking, he had bags under his eyes, like he hadn't slept. He was quiet and reserved.

I usually wished a condemned man good luck, because they often had appeals still pending. But this time I didn't know what to say. My eyes were stinging, and I felt like I was going to cry. But there was no way in hell I could.

Larry Fitzgerald

Napoleon had been on death row almost as long as I'd been at TDCJ. The first time I saw him, I was amazed at how young he looked. It was his age that bothered me most: he was a kid of 17, who couldn't vote or buy liquor or cigarettes when he committed the crime, yet he was old enough to be executed. After they locked him up in county jail, I heard he wouldn't sleep on the bunk, he'd sleep on the floor instead. I think that was him trying to punish himself. When death row was at the Ellis Unit and they gave the offenders jobs, they made him a porter. That tells you that he was somebody the warden could trust. He was like his mom and dad raised him, was always polite and followed every order.

He was what we call in the prison system 'a good convict-citizen'. He deserved a second chance.

On the day of his execution, me and Michelle went back there to take him through the process and I suddenly had this feeling that he needed to write out a last statement, rather than mutter a few words on the gurney, because he was such a smart person. So I said to him, 'If you've got something you want to say, write out what's in your heart and I'll make sure it's transcribed and handed out after this thing is over.' He agreed. Then, just before we left, I turned to him and said, 'Napoleon, you look pretty calm.' He replied, 'Look again.' I shook his hand and left, but I was never able to flush that final conversation out of my mind. The next time I saw him, he was on the gurney with straps all over him. I had some pretty strong feelings about it. Napoleon's death had a profound effect on me. He was my friend. I was sad to see him go, and getting awfully tired of executions...

Later that afternoon, I had to type up Napoleon's statement for the media. He'd written it in less than an hour, but it was so sincere and an impressive piece of penmanship. As I was typing, I was hoping he'd get a stay, because I didn't want to see him die, while feeling guilty for thinking that way. It was a complex day. The Board of Pardons and Parole usually voted unanimously not to commute an inmate's sentence to life imprisonment or grant a reprieve, but in Napoleon's case they voted 10–7 and

13–4 respectively, which showed they were still deeply divided. Then news came in that the Supreme Court had voted 6–0 against staying Napoleon's execution.

I didn't have any choice but to hold my emotions in check, because that was the first time Larry had let me do a press conference, and I didn't want to let him down. We didn't have a press conference after most executions, because there wasn't enough media interest, and when we did, they were usually small affairs held inside. But because there was so much media in town for Napoleon, we set up a podium outside. All the media from Tyler County was down, national newspapers, and I was going out live on CNN, so it wouldn't have looked good if I'd started weeping. I typed up a skeleton script, leaving out details to be filled in later – time pronounced dead, last statement, demeanour – and headed to the death chamber. And while Napoleon was dying on the gurney, at the age of 25, I was making notes...

'stoic, didn't look up... when asked if he had a statement, "no, no"... closed his eyes, coughed several times... never opened eyes – small smile? 10 coughs – head lifted off gurney during 3.'

Michelle's notes on the execution of Napoleon Beazley, 28 May 2002

Napoleon Beazley's written last statement

The act I committed to put me here was not just heinous, it was senseless. But the person that committed that act is no longer here – I am.

I'm not going to struggle physically against any restraints. I'm not going to shout, use profanity or make idle threats. Understand though that I'm not only upset, but I'm saddened by what is happening here tonight. I'm not only saddened, but disappointed that a system that is supposed to protect and uphold what is just and right can be so much like me when I made the same shameful mistake.

If someone tried to dispose of everyone here for participating in this killing, I'd scream a resounding, 'No.' I'd tell them to give them all the gift that they would not give me... and that's to give them all a second chance.

I'm sorry that I am here. I'm sorry that you're all here. I'm sorry that John Luttig died. And I'm sorry that it was something in me that caused all of this to happen to begin with.

Tonight, we tell the world that there are no second chances in the eyes of justice... Tonight, we tell our children that in some instances, in some cases, killing is right.

This conflict hurts us all, there are no SIDES. The people who support this proceeding think this is justice. The people that think that I should live think that is justice. As difficult as it may seem, this is a clash of ideals, with both parties committed to what they feel is right. But who's wrong if in the end we're all victims?

In my heart, I have to believe that there is a peaceful compromise to our ideals. I don't mind if there are none for me, as long as there are for those who are yet to come. There are a lot of men like me on death row – good men – who fell to the same misguided emotions, but may not have recovered as I have.

Give those men a chance to do what's right. Give them a chance to undo their wrongs. A lot of them want to fix the mess they started, but don't know how. The problem is not in that people aren't willing to help them find out, but in the system telling them it won't matter anyway.

No-one wins tonight. No-one gets closure. No-one walks away victorious.

CHAPTER 8
MAYBE THE PAIN WILL STOP

'You know what my worst nightmare is? That you'll take me over to the death house and kill me and I'll wake up the next day and be back here on death row.'

Thomas Miller-El, former death row inmate

'I haven't much patience with people who say our laws are barbaric.'

John B. Holmes Jr, former Harris County District Attorney

After watching Napoleon die, I cried all the way home. I thought I'd just witnessed a fundamentally good man be executed. I'd gotten too close. At least nobody knew how I was feeling, although, in hindsight, I wish they'd at least had an inkling. If the letters and emails had been scathing before Napoleon's stay in 2001, this time they were on another level. Because I was now working for the prison system, I really shouldn't have replied to any of them, but I couldn't help myself. Here I was struggling with Napoleon's execution and I was being attacked for being a heartless bitch. I thought, 'You don't know me, and you have no idea what's going on inside my head.' Nobody knew what was going on inside my head, not even me.

A pastor wrote to me from Germany, urging me 'not to sponsor this death row machinery by doing this ugly job any more'. I was mad as hell and gave him both barrels, told him that I was amazed a man of God could be so 'caustic and hateful'. Someone from Norway told me I should be 'denouncing the shame and barbarity' of the death penalty, rather than standing by and watching men die. I replied, 'I don't how anyone can have so much nerve as to lecture a complete stranger. YOU HAVE NO RIGHT.' I received a spidery, handwritten letter from a man named Gregory in Athlone, Ireland, who told me how 'disgusted' he was that I 'took pleasure' from watching executions. He signed off by inviting me over for a holiday. I knew the Irish were hospitable, but not *that* hospitable. Because CNN finally screened the interview Christiane Amanpour (*fuck* Christiane Amanpour!) did with me the previous year, in which I said I received a lot of poisonous letters and emails, I also got quite a few supportive messages. But even some of these managed to upset me, including one that stated Napoleon 'got what was coming to him', and another from a woman in the UK, who compared Napoleon to the British serial killers Myra Hindley and Rose West. Other people would be very nice, before letting themselves down by asking what I was wearing.

A month after Napoleon was executed, Robert Coulson was scheduled to die. Coulson was convicted of murdering five members of his family, as well as an unborn baby, in Houston in 1992. Coulson apparently suffocated his victims with plastic bags and trussed them all up, before setting the house on fire, so that he could claim a $600,000 inheritance. He always maintained the police planted evidence at the scene, but an accomplice immediately confessed and Coulson's protests fell on deaf ears. We talked whenever I was on death row and he said to me once, 'It's like you bring sunshine with you.' Whatever he was supposed to have done, he seemed very nice, and that was a sweet thing for him to say. Right before his execution, he wrote me a letter that started, 'If you're reading this, they killed me…' It arrived a few days later and was a kind letter, but while I was reading it, I was thinking, 'This is crazy, I just watched this guy die…'

One letter that really bothered me was from Gerald Mitchell, who robbed and shot to death two men in Houston in 1985. Mitchell apologised for not having made a better impression on me, which made me feel awful. I hadn't thought bad of him at all, I just thought he was nervous. Reading his letter, which was written in the most elaborate, almost gothic, handwriting, I thought, 'You had so many other things to worry about, you shouldn't have been worrying about that.' I wished I had received that letter before he was executed, so that I could have gotten word to him that he came across just fine.

Because I seemed happy, I wasn't like the people the inmates were normally around. I guess I was like a little shard of light in their otherwise grim lives. These were men who weren't allowed to touch anybody, the only physical contact they had was when they were being escorted and two officers had their hands on their elbows. It wasn't meant to be punitive or cruel, it was because these men had nothing to lose.

Before Martin Gurule's breakout, death row inmates weren't much different from the general population. They lived two to a cell, had a work programme, went to church, had television, ate in the mess hall with all the other prisoners. There was a day room at the Ellis Unit, where inmates could socialise. There were televisions on the walls opposite their cells, so they could watch the Astros play baseball or the Cowboys play football. They could play chess, on boards hung from their cell doors by string, and dominoes, on blankets laid out in the walkways. But when they moved all the condemned men to Polunsky, everything was locked down. That's why it was known as one of the hardest places to do time in Texas.

If they behaved, they'd be allowed a radio, a typewriter and one hour's recreation a day. They'd also be allowed newspaper and magazine subscriptions, unless they contained pictures of naked women or instructions on how to escape from prison. There was also a library, so you could check out books. If they didn't behave so well, they'd lose the radio and get three or four hours' recreation a week. Thomas Mason once told me that if they'd been allowed TV on death row, they would have been better behaved, because knowing you might get your TV taken away is a whole different ball game to losing a radio. If they behaved real bad, they'd only be allowed legal materials in their cell and one hour's recreation a week. But even when they were out of their cell, they still wouldn't be able to touch anybody else. You'd see them playing 'horse', which is a basketball game where you make a shot and the other person makes the same shot from the exact same position, standing on one leg or whatever you may choose. The two inmates would have this big chain fence between them, but it was intimacy of sorts. Some of the guys had chess boards, and they'd play their neighbour by calling out their moves. Sometimes they'd lie on the floor and chat through the gap under the door. But most of them just sat and waited in their cells, flexing idle fingers.

Stephen Moody, who was sentenced in 1993 for shooting a man to death, summed it up: 'Have you ever been to the zoo and looked into the eyes of the animals they have caged there? If so, you couldn't help but have noticed the pain and confusion. All the pacing back and forth in the cage gets the animal nowhere, he just becomes a little more confused as each year passes, losing more and more of himself as he goes…' Moody was executed more than nine years later, on 16 September 2009.

Once, when the officers were searching the cells for contraband, they found a little jar full of baby black widow spiders. The inmate had been trying to figure out a way to milk them for their venom, so he could put it on the tip of a spear and stab an officer with it. Michael McBride, who was considered strange even by the standards of death row, tried to procure a shampoo bottle and some jalapeño seeds, so he could squirt the juice into the eyes of anyone who happened to be annoying him, which, by the sounds of it, was everyone. That's what happens when you have no real incentive to behave and are going slowly mad in a tiny cell with a slit of a window for years, if you weren't mad already. And that's why we were always being warned to be careful around the inmates. If they weren't planning to harm someone else, they might be planning to harm themselves, like Andre Thomas, who gouged out his own eye and ate it, having already gouged out the other in county jail, before he landed on death row.

On the outside of each cell would be little markers, so if a guy was an escapist, he'd have an 'ES' sticker. There was a sticker for assault, a sticker for cutting, and some cells would be lit up with these stickers. One day, I was standing outside with the media, supervising some filming, and this guy was brought out in a wheelchair, with a spear sticking out of his neck. He was holding it, very calmly, but all I could think was, 'Oh my God, they're gonna run him into the door...' Then I thought, 'I cannot possibly let the reporters see this.' Somehow, the guy was whisked away in a car without any of the reporters seeming to notice. He was a contractor, fitting cameras on death row, and inmates don't like cameras. So one of them harpooned him with a spear made out of tightly-rolled paper and an improvised tip, probably a bit of metal broken off a bunk.

Another inmate, named Robert Pruett, landed himself on death row for stabbing a correctional officer to death with a shank at another unit, apparently because the officer had written an unfavourable report on him. Often when something like that happened, it would transpire that an officer had done something to upset the inmate months earlier. The officer would forget about the incident, but the inmate wouldn't. He'd be sitting in his cell, nursing his grievance, until he spotted an opportunity to exact retribution.

Most of the inmates were just desperate for some contact with the outside world. Because they had no TV, they couldn't see what people were wearing, and because the signal wasn't great at Polunsky, they listened mostly to a local station out of Livingston.

People would call in and give shout-outs to inmates, which was a very niche market. Randy Arroyo, this funny young Hispanic guy out of San Antonio, used to come to visitation wearing sweatbands around his head and wrists, as if he was in *Flashdance*. When he went in, it must have been a cool look, but it wasn't as if I was going to tell him fashion had moved on.

Many of the inmates had no concept of cell phones or the internet, they were these grey-haired men, completely out of touch. Their experience of the real world stopped the day they were locked up. But a lot of the younger ones signed up to special websites, devoted to matching them with pen pals. While the inmates had no access to computers, they had no shortage of friends outside, willing to create these pages on their behalf, and those pen pals were their link to the free world. The inmates would ask for magazines or newspapers, or for money to be put on their books, so they could purchase commissary. Farley Matchett, who beat two people to death with a hammer in 1991, one of them in Huntsville, was pen pals with Brigitte Bardot. Gregory Summers corresponded with schoolchildren in Italy. Why their teacher, who wanted Summers to be buried in Pisa, thought they should write letters to a man who stabbed his adoptive parents to death is anyone's guess.

A few inmates used blogs to flex their creative muscles, display their literary prowess and try to make some kind of sense of why they wound up on death row. When Thomas Bartlett Whitaker told his parents he'd finished his final exams and graduated from

Sam Houston State, they presented him with a Rolex watch and took him out for a celebratory dinner. When they arrived home, Whitaker's mom and brother were shot dead by an intruder. He and his dad were also shot, but both survived.

It transpired that not only had Whitaker not graduated, he wasn't even enrolled at Sam Houston State. It also transpired that Whitaker had planned the murders. At the trial, Whitaker's dad pleaded for his son's life, to no avail. I felt so sad for that poor man. On death row, Whitaker wrote extensively about his experiences in a blog called Minutes Before Six, which at first was maintained by his father, and then by friends on the outside. He'd get other inmates to write stories or poetry, but it was mainly his work. There was also some lighter stuff, including recipes. He talked about making *tamales*, a traditional Mexican dish, using a bag of mashed-up potato chips and tinned tuna. It sounded nasty, but it gave an insight into how ingenious some of these inmates were.

Whitaker won all sorts of prison awards for his work, which only made the whole thing sadder. Like Napoleon, he could have done great things, but he destroyed lives instead, including his own. Unlike Napoleon, Whitaker was described by those who knew him as a stone-cold sociopath.

'If a person could hear their own coffin being closed over them, it would sound like a cell door. I remember standing at that door, taking in my new 10ft by 6ft cage, which would become my retirement home – where I would spend my

golden years...'

Thomas Whitaker, Minutes Before Six, 24 July 2007

Other death row inmates didn't just want a pen pal, they wanted a wife. I was fascinated by these women who claimed to have fallen in love, came over from Europe and married some guy who had killed a bunch of people. They'd get one long visit a month, so they'd come at the end of August, for example, and stay until the first week of September, to combine two visits in one trip. In some cases, Amnesty International paid for them, so it was almost as if their job was to be a death row wife. I interviewed one, for a feature I planned to write, and she reckoned the attraction was the fact it was a 'safe' relationship: she hardly ever saw her husband, there was no physical contact, he couldn't cheat on her, and therefore couldn't break her heart. And, let's be honest, it's easier to get a date with a man on death row than out in the real world. The relationship was very intense, because all his attention was on her, but he couldn't do anything to harm her. Bizarre. The sick thing was, some inmates still managed to be unfaithful. One time, two girlfriends turned up at the same time and things got explosive. Proof that if someone really wants to cheat, they'll find a way.

These relationships would have been quite sweet if they were genuine, but I questioned some of the wives' motives. They'd often turn up to witness executions and wail and throw themselves on the floor, and it would look like a show. One wife from Germany refused to put her shoes on, because she thought it would halt the execution. We made it clear we would carry on the execution without her. I'd feel sorry for the victims' families, or for those who were watching a son or brother die, while these women were going through the death throes of their 15 minutes of fame. Another time, a wife had this big argument with the inmate's mom in the witness room, because his mom wanted to claim his body and his wife wanted to bury him in Europe. These wives barely knew their husbands, had never even touched them. All they'd ever done was write letters back and forth.

But one inmate who did have a genuine relationship was George Rivas, a particularly rough convict out of El Paso. Rivas was the leader of a gang nicknamed 'The Texas Seven', who pulled off the biggest prison escape in the state's history in 2001. The inmates were working in an industrial plant at the Connally Unit in Kenedy when they overpowered some workers, stole their clothes, broke into the prison armoury and drove right out of there. Rivas left a note: 'You haven't heard the last of us yet.' While on the run, they committed a ton of robberies and appeared on *America's Most Wanted*, before shooting to death a police officer, who stumbled across them robbing a sporting goods store in Dallas. They made it all the way to Colorado before they were apprehended, but not before one had killed himself rather than be taken back into custody.

Because they couldn't determine who killed the police officer – he was shot 11 times – it was a Law of Parties case, which basically

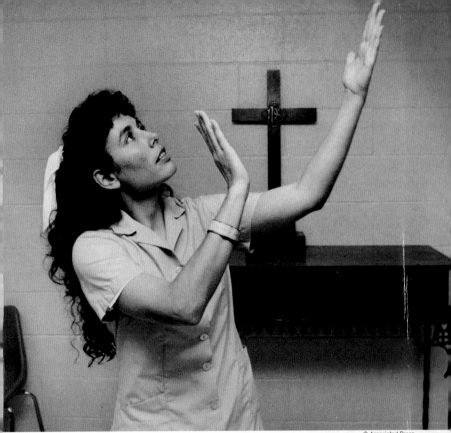

Karla Faye Tucker murdered two people with a pickaxe in Houston in 1983, but found God on death row. Larry considered her a friend and felt bereft when she became the first woman to be executed since the Civil War, in 1998.

Napoleon Beazley was just 17 when he murdered John Luttig, the father of a federal judge. After I joined the Texas Department of Criminal Justice as a spokesperson in 2001, I got to know and like him, almost as a friend.

Because of Napoleon's age at the time of his crime, his death sentence caused a global outcry. The United States was one of only five countries to execute 'juveniles', the others being Saudi Arabia, Iran, Congo and Nigeria.

EXECUTION RECORDING

OFFENDER: Beazley, Napoleon #999141

EXECUTION DATE: May 28, 2002

TAKEN FROM HOLDING CELL   _6:01_   TIME

STRAPPED TO GURNEY   _6:02_   TIME

SOLUTION FLOWING   _6:04_   RIGHT HAND/ARM

_6:04_   LEFT HAND/ARM

LAST STATEMENT   _6:07_ TIME

LETHAL DOSE BEGAN   _6:08_ TIME

LETHAL DOSE COMPLETED   _6:12_   TIME

PRONOUNCED DEAD   _6:17_   TIME

UNUSUAL
OCCURRENCES:_____

_____

_____

_____

_____

_____

After receiving one stay of execution, Napoleon was put to death on
28 May 2002. While he slipped away on the gurney, I was writing
notes in the witness room. That was a tough day for Larry and me.

Larry got on well with many death row inmates, but thought Kenneth Allen McDuff was a monster. McDuff, who killed as many as 16 people, is the only offender to have been sent to Texas death row twice.

Jim Brazzil – or, as Larry liked to call him, The Sinister Minister – was the Walls Unit chaplain, who ministered to the spiritual needs of condemned men in their final hours. His Bible was signed by some of Texas' most notorious criminals.

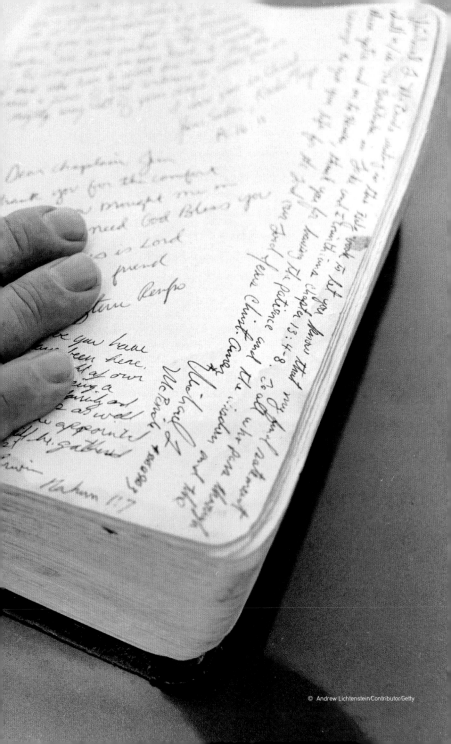

boilerplate© Andrew Lichtenstein/Contributor/Getty

LAST MEAL REQUEST
LAWRENCE RUSSELL BREWER #999327
SEPTEMBER 21, 2011

(2) Chicken Fried Steaks smothered in gravy w/sliced onions

Triple meat bacon cheeseburger w/fixings on side

Cheese omelet w/ground beef, tomatoes, onions, bell and jalapenos

Large bowl fried okra w/ketchup

(1) pound of BBQ w/half loaf white bread

(3) Fajitas w/fixings w/1 pint of Blue Bell Homemade Vanilla

Pizza Meat Lovers Special w/3 root beers

Slab of peanut butter fudge w/crushed peanuts

When Lawrence Brewer was scheduled to die in 2011, for his part in the Jasper dragging case 13 years earlier, his request of a bountiful last meal inadvertently led to the decades-old custom being discontinued.

George Rivas was the leader of 'The Texas Seven', who pulled off the biggest prison escape in the state's history in 2001, before killing a cop. Rivas was a rough individual, but I wept after watching him die.

Larry and I enjoy a night out at a favourite dive bar. Larry was my mentor and taught me everything I know about being a good spokesperson. He was also a wonderful man and I miss him greatly.

Peckerwood Hill has been the last stop for Texas inmates since the 1850s and about 3,000 are buried there, including some of the most dangerous men and women in the state's history. It is a sad and lonely place, with a certain beauty.

The Joe Byrd Cemetery, colloquially known as
Peckerwood Hill, is where prisoners who die in the
system and aren't claimed by their families are buried.
The stones of executed inmates are marked with an 'X'.

means you can be convicted of murder even if it wasn't you who pulled the trigger. It was often controversial, because it meant people were sentenced to death who hadn't actually murdered anyone. For example, Thomas Bartlett Whitaker was sentenced to death for planning the murders of his mother and brother, but the person he hired to kill them got a life sentence instead. But in Rivas' case it made some kind of sense. All six ended up on death row, and Rivas was the second to be executed.

The death row officers told me that while he was awaiting trial, Rivas began receiving letters from a freelance journalist. She'd seen him in the news, something about him intrigued her, and they developed a relationship – she attended almost of all the trial, and they married shortly after he arrived at Polunsky. The officers told me she was cute as could be, had her shit together and seemed like a normal person. She moved close to the Polunsky Unit, so she could see him every week, and they got married: Rivas signed off on his consent, the bride took the paperwork to the courthouse, and what you might call a 'stunt groom' stood in for Rivas. Eventually they divorced, because, according to Rivas, she decided she couldn't handle watching him die.

When Rivas was asked at his trial about the motive for the escape, he replied, 'I wasn't going to die an old man in prison.' I couldn't really blame him. For the same reason, there were men who ordered that no more appeals be filed by their lawyer and volunteered for execution, including one of Rivas' accomplices,

Michael Rodriguez. It was strange to me that there were all these defence lawyers running around, filing appeals and coming up with all these bizarre arguments, when they knew their clients were guilty and just wanted to die.

> 'The hardest thing for me was to look in a mirror for
> 13 years and know I took a life. The memory haunts me.
> I say put me on the gurney and maybe the pain will stop.'
>
> **Jeffery Tucker, executed on 14 November 2001**

One guy was in the holding cell at the death house, all prepared, resigned to the fact he was going to die, and when I told him that his lawyer had won him a stay of execution, he got really upset and said, 'This just means there's gonna be six more months of this shit.' I understood that most of these defence lawyers were good people, anti-death penalty to the core and fighting these cases on principle, but the reality was that Texas had the death penalty, and some of their clients didn't want to be saved, because they didn't want to be in prison any more. Like Napoleon said, living with a death sentence was like living with a terminal disease. Maybe that's why there was compassion between death row inmates, the likes of which was rare among the general population. These little acts of charity between dying men were reminders that life, however awful, retained some beauty...

What's in the brown paper bag?
By Luis Ramirez

'I'm about to share with you a story whose telling is long past due. It's a familiar story to most of you reading this from death row. And now it's one that all of you in "free world" may benefit from. This is the story of my first day on the row.

'I came here in May of 1999. The exact date is something that I can't recall. I do remember arriving in the afternoon. I was placed in a cell on H-20 wing over at the Ellis Unit in Huntsville. A tsunami of emotions and thoughts were going through my mind at the time. I remember the only things in the cell were a mattress, pillow, a couple of sheets, a pillowcase, a roll of toilet paper, and a blanket. I remember sitting there, utterly lost.

'The first person I met there was Napoleon Beazley. Back then, death row prisoners still worked. His job at the time was to clean up the wing and help serve during meal times. He was walking around sweeping the pod in these ridiculous looking rubber boots. He came up to the bars on my cell and asked me if I was new. I told him that I had just arrived on death row.

'He asked what my name is. I told him, not seeing any harm in it. He then stepped back where he could see all three tiers. He hollered at everyone, "There's a new man here. He just drove up. His name is Luis Ramirez." When he did that, I didn't know what to make of it at first. I thought I had made some kind of mistake.

'You see, like most of you, I was of the impression that everyone on death row was evil. I thought I would find hundreds of Hannibal Lecters *in here. And now, they all knew my name. I thought, "Oh well, that's strike one." I was sure that they would soon begin harassing me. This is what happens in the movies after all.*

'Well, that's not what happened. After supper was served, Napoleon was once again sweeping the floors. As he passed my cell, he swept a brown paper bag into it. I asked him, "What's this?" He said for me to look inside and continued on his way. Man, I didn't know what to expect. I was certain it was something bad. Curiosity did get the best of me though. I carefully opened the bag. What I found was the last thing I ever expected to find on death row, and everything I needed.

'The bag contained some stamps, envelopes, notepad, pen, soap, shampoo, toothpaste, tooth brush, a pastry, a soda, and a couple of Ramen noodles. I remember asking Napoleon where this came from. He told me that everyone had pitched in. That they knew that I didn't have anything and that it may be a while before I could get them. I asked him to find out who had contributed. I wanted to pay them back. He said, "It's not like that. Just remember the next time you see someone come here like you. You pitch in something."

'I sat there on my bunk with my brown paper bag of goodies, and thought about what had just happened to me. The last things I expected to find on death row was kindness and generosity. They knew what I needed and they took it upon themselves to meet those needs. They did this without any expectation of reimbursement or compensation. They did this for a stranger, not a known friend. I don't know what they felt when they committed this act of incredible kindness.

'I only know that like them, twelve "good people" had deemed me beyond redemption. The only remedy that these "good people" could offer us is death. Somehow what these "good people" saw and what I was seeing didn't add up. How could these men, who just showed me so much humanity, be considered the "worst of the worst"?

'Ever since Napoleon was executed, for a crime he committed as a teen, I've wanted to share this story with his family. I would like for them to know that their son was a good man. One who I will never forget. I want for them to know how sorry I am that we as a society failed them and him.

'I still find it ridiculous that we as a people feel that we cannot teach or love our young properly. I'm appalled at the idea that a teen is beyond redemption, that the only solution that we can offer is death. It's tragic that this is being pointed out to the "good people" by one of the "worst of the worst". God help us all.

'What's in the brown paper bag? I found caring, kindness, love, humanity, and compassion of a scale that I've never seen the "good people" in the free world show towards one another.'

Luis Ramirez was executed on 20 October 2005, for the murder of Nemecio Nandin in Tennyson on 8 April 1998.

CHAPTER 9
A HORRIBLE PLACE TO BE

'It wasn't difficult. I was kind of looking forward to it.'

Erick Martinez, on the execution of his mother's killer Luis Salazar

'The only closure I could feel is if my son comes knocking on my door and says I'm home.'

Donald Whittington Jr, on the execution of his son's killer Justin Fuller

Larry Fitzgerald, Larry Todd and Glen Castlebury quit on the same day in 2003, because all three qualified for a retirement incentive that was just too good an offer to pass up. But I thought Fitzgerald wasn't ready to retire. His mother was very old (she lived to be over 100) and he spent a lot of time looking after her. Their relationship was very cute. He used to take her to baseball games and put her in a little Houston Astros cap. But Larry was still young and wasn't the stay-at-home, putter-around-the-garden type. Almost immediately, he started doing work for the Office of Emergency Management, and wild fires and hurricanes were right up his alley. But he was no longer on the front line, and I think he missed dealing with reporters and all the banter that went with it. Larry was smart, and crime reporters are smart, talking to them is not like talking to your average Joe Blow in a store.

I loved working with him and he taught me so much. Every single thing journalists complimented me about – about how open or helpful I was – I learned from Larry. He taught me what was needed to be successful in that job. For example, when I first started at TDCJ, I was petrified to do radio interviews. Television didn't bother me at all, but radio freaked me out, because I was worried I wasn't giving them good soundbites. For a while, I avoided it at all costs. But I listened to Larry and picked things up, and actually became pretty good at it. He would still offer me advice after he left, although I never asked for it, because I was young and headstrong and didn't want to appear weak.

I'd see him and his wife every few months, when I was attending board meetings in Austin, and we'd chat about the old days. He'd send me funny emails and articles he'd read, often about upcoming executions and what he saw as the vagaries and absurdities of the prison system. He'd call at 5.45 p.m., knowing full well that we had an execution in 15 minutes, and say, 'Hey, what's going on? Is Graczyk there? You know, gal, what you need to do is this, this and this...' He was missing it and just trying to help, but it drove me nuts. I'd say, 'I know, Larry, I know!' It was like talking to a parent, so frustrating. But I missed him terribly, because I loved him dearly. Everybody loved him, even the inmates, which tells you everything. Larry never stopped being the face of TDCJ, and always will be.

Larry Fitzgerald

I never thought I'd work for the prison system and I never thought I'd retire from the prison system, but both of those things happened. Those first two years at TDCJ were a fun existence. Employees of the Texas prison system were often portrayed as knuckle-draggers, but that wasn't the case. There were some people who wouldn't have fit in anywhere, but the vast majority were just doing a job, and carried out their jobs with a great deal of respect. I made a lot of friends in Huntsville and have fond memories of the place. But it got to the stage where I thought, 'This has gone on for way too long.'

I was always asked by the media, 'Do you support the death penalty?' I always dodged the question by replying, 'It's not germane to the story whether I do or don't.' I had to play it straight down the middle, because if I'd said I was against it, I'd have lost all the families of the victims; and if I'd said I was for it, I'd have lost a whole bunch of offenders on death row. Mike Graczyk had seen far more executions than me and I never knew what his view of the death penalty was either. That's the way it had to be, and that's what made him such a good reporter. The truth was, I did still support the death penalty. You can't know somebody like Kenneth Allen McDuff and say you're against it. And had I been on the jury at Napoleon's trial, I would have voted for the death penalty as well. I got to know Napoleon real well, and thought the world of him, but the jurors just thought he was a monster.

I got to think that Texas was using the death penalty way too much. There were some people we executed who could have served a life sentence instead. There were a few people we executed I thought might be innocent. But I also came to realise that everybody is a victim at an execution: the offender, the offender's family, the actual victim's family. I always maintained that there was no such thing as closure when related to the death penalty. Seeing the person who killed your loved one die might bring some immediate satisfaction, but it's just the start of another chapter in an ugly story. I took a lot of heat from victims' families for saying that publicly. But I just didn't think anything was accomplished by executing somebody.

I grew weary of seeing women collapsing in the witness room, pounding the glass and kicking the wall. I vividly recall the mother of Larry Robison doing exactly that. Robison committed one of the most horrible crimes you could imagine. In Fort Worth in 1982, Rickey Bryant's mother paid her son a visit and found him dead on the kitchen floor, his head hacked off and placed under his arm. His penis was found in the kitchen sink. Next door, four more victims had been stabbed and shot to death, including an 11-year-old boy. Robison was picked up the very next day. On the day of his execution, in January 2000, his mother really gave me grief: 'You're murdering my son!' Robison was supposed to be the crazy one, but his mother was worse. That was pretty hard to take, but I couldn't help but feel sorry for her.

There were other things I saw in the death chamber that were just plain frightening. One inmate stockpiled his medication and tried to commit suicide in his cell the day before his execution. They flew him down to the prison hospital in Galveston, pumped his stomach full of charcoal to flush out the poison, and flew him back to Huntsville, so they could kill him. I thought that was pretty ironic. When they strapped him to the gurney, he started projectile vomiting in purple and I thought he was having a haemorrhage. It came on the heels of an execution in Florida, when they'd used a synthetic sponge and the offender's head had caught on fire, so I was standing there thinking, 'Now we've got our *own disaster. What the hell am I gonna tell the media?' After he was executed, I ran into Wayne Scott, the executive director, and he told me that the offender had drunk a cup of punch in the holding cell and it had reacted with the charcoal, which was still in his stomach. At least I had my story. Things like that you don't forget in a hurry, but it was the executions I couldn't remember that bothered me most; the executions without drama; the executions that nobody showed up to watch. Those offenders died and nobody even noticed. That's a sad thought.*

Michelle is right, I did miss it for a few months. I enjoyed most of my job and think I did my job well. I was paid to tell people what went down in the prisons of Huntsville, and that's what I did, because I thought they had a right to know. But after a while, I cannot tell you how happy I was to be gone. Prison is a horrible place to be. It changes men and takes its toll. I'd witnessed 219 executions and didn't want to see another – except perhaps for one. I always told Michelle I wanted to come back to witness the execution of John William King, the white supremacist ring leader in the murder of James Byrd Jr in Jasper. It was such a horrible crime, King was such a horrible man and a real asshole to deal with. We never got along, and I just felt like I needed to witness that one last execution to close the chapter for me. Unfortunately, he's still alive and well on death row...

'I couldn't talk to many people about my role, and no other chaplain knew what was going on in my head. But I had two or three close friends that I could really unload on, Larry being one of them. There wasn't a day that went by when we didn't talk. He was always there, with his crazy ideas and gallows humour. But he was also a professional and had great integrity. There was no better advocate for the inmates than Larry.

'People hated us because we worked for the prison system. Over the years, I got a whole lot of death threats, but I would not have had Larry's job for anything. He had a difficult balance, telling the truth but telling it delicately. He became known as the face of executions in Texas, while dealing with his own ambivalence towards the death penalty.

'Larry took a lot of heat, and the struggle with life and death was hard on him. His mom was ill, he had a brother-in-law who was pretty sick, and he let his guard down at work. One day he'd be sharing a joke with an inmate, the next day that inmate would be dead.

'Larry and I talked about life and death and his own mortality on many occasions. It affected him a great deal, and he drank a lot. And when Larry broke down and cried, I did, too.'

Jim Brazzil, former Huntsville Unit chaplain

I got married in Mexico in September 2003, and while I was on my honeymoon, Larry Todd's replacement started in the job. The expectation was that I would take over the running of the public information office, that's what they were grooming me for, but the guy they hired was a little bit older and had stronger Republican connections in the Governor's office than I did. I was told I'd be promoted to Fitzgerald's old job instead, but the first time I met this new guy, I knew he was trouble. We were at a prison board meeting when he said, 'Hey, I'm your new boss.' Right off the bat, he was obnoxious. He knew I'd interviewed for that job and it had come down to the two of us.

The following week, we had a meeting, and the first thing he said was, 'Yeah, I'm not gonna promote you.' I asked him why not, and he said, 'I didn't like what you had on at the board meeting. It wasn't professional.' I was wearing khaki pants and this badass shirt from a cool boutique, but he thought I should have been more dressed up. I said, 'Fortunately, that's not your call, I will walk before I let you do that to me,' stormed out and slammed the door behind me.

I got on the phone to the executive director and asked him what the hell was going on. He said, 'Yeah, I knew he was gonna do that. I told him that if you cursed at him or anything like that, I'd support him, but if you didn't, I wouldn't.' It had been a test and I was livid. I replied, 'Let me tell you right now, he's gonna put the nail in his own coffin. You just watch.' The executive director told me he hoped I'd help my new boss succeed, to which I replied, 'Sure, I'll help him, but it's not going to change anything.' They let my promotion go through, but the process left a sour taste.

*

In 1995, former Beaumont police officer and sheriff's deputy Hilton Crawford kidnapped and murdered a 12-year-old boy, the only child of his old friends in Conroe. The boy called Crawford 'Uncle Hilty', that's how close they were. Crawford had no prior criminal convictions, but his security business had collapsed and he'd got himself in a lot of financial trouble, which led to him kidnapping the boy and demanding a ransom. When his parents realised the boy was missing, Crawford was one of the first people they called, because of his experience in law enforcement and because they considered him that good a friend. A few days later, the boy's blood was found inside the trunk of Crawford's car before the body turned up in Louisiana. In the wake of the child's murder, his mom had a stroke and she and her husband divorced.

On death row, Crawford's fellow inmates didn't call him 'Uncle Hilty', they called him 'Old Man'. Just before Larry retired, Crawford, now 64, was scheduled to be executed. He said he'd trade everything in his last meal request for some catfish, but they didn't have it in the kitchen. So I thought, 'You know what? I bet the store down the street has some.' I went down there, paid seven dollars for some catfish and told the clerk he couldn't tell anybody. He said he understood, and would want somebody to do that for him if he was being executed.

I took the fish to the warden, and he said he'd make sure it got to Brian Price in the kitchen, so he could fry it up. But the warden was also slightly bemused, and asked, 'What on earth would make you want to do that?' I paused for a moment, before replying, 'Because if this is the one food item this man has missed since he's been in prison, the least I can do is make sure he gets it, even if he doesn't deserve it.' But afterwards, I was racked with guilt. What was I thinking? He killed a child. What is wrong with you? I was also terrified he was going to mention it on the gurney: 'Miss Lyons, thank you for the catfish, that was very kind of you...' He did talk about it when he first entered the chamber, but not in his last statement, thank God. Nobody had any idea, which is why the catfish doesn't appear in official prison records. But I never did it again, because I was so ashamed and embarrassed.

At the same time as I was beginning to churn up inside, I was continuing to project a tough image. I still made fun of people who got emotional at executions, including one reporter from the *Houston Chronicle*, who wrote that it was the most devastating thing she'd ever seen and had ended up in therapy. I thought, 'Jesus, you're a fucking journalist, this is a pretty basic thing you're covering, you should be able to do it without cracking up. You are such a baby!'

I really did have contempt for these people. There was a certain amount of smugness because I was a woman who could handle it and thought myself so much tougher than all these female reporters queuing up to cry in the bathroom. TDCJ was a macho environment, made up mostly of men, and I was usually the only woman backstage before an execution. Women were automatically seen as weaker creatures, so I was determined to show my colleagues that wasn't necessarily the case.

My stop–start promotion was proof that I'd have to work much harder to get the same respect as a man performing the same role, but they didn't want to pay me the same as they paid the men. A newspaper ran a story, comparing the salaries of all the state government public information officers, and it revealed that me and another woman, from the Texas Department of Public Safety, were the lowest-paid. At the time, TDCJ had 38,000 employees, 75,000 parolees and 150,000 inmates, and I spoke on behalf of all of those people. But I was earning less than the spokesman for the Texas Youth Commission, the prison system for juvenile delinquents. And because he claimed he couldn't give out details on a minor, he regularly shrugged off media requests. So my bosses knew, and they didn't do a goddamn thing about it. I'm sure they thought they were being progressive by giving me a job at all.

I can't tell you how many inappropriate comments I heard working for TDCJ, and there were a few male co-workers I needed to worry about more than the inmates. I was driving back from one of the units with a colleague, mentioned I had a bad headache and he reached over and started rubbing the back of my neck. Instead of saying, 'What the fuck are you doing?' I tensed up, got all embarrassed and said, 'You know what, it's better all of a sudden...' That happened twice, and I'm pissed I didn't confront him. Another time, I was on a unit with a warden, we walked past a cell with some mattresses in it and he stopped and said, 'You want to throw one of those mattresses down and fool around?' I liked this guy, so I laughed it off. I didn't want to be the uncool lady who complained about 'harmless banter'. But I was also thinking, 'Oh my God, I could have your job in a heartbeat...' Then again, probably not.

I'd go to meetings and all the men would hug me. I didn't want all those men hugging me. Why didn't they just shake my hand, like they did with other men? That kind of shit drove me nuts, but I never lamented my lot, I just had to play the game, because I wouldn't have lasted long if I hadn't.

The reporters soon started calling my new boss 'no comment', because he just didn't want to deal with them. He refused to go to any of the prison units, which made him obsolete, because that's where the reporters would be. And reporters don't take kindly to being fobbed off by email. He buried his head in admin, budget stuff that would only come into play every two years. I was setting up interviews, doing female death row every Tuesday and male death row every Wednesday, and the reporters started asking exactly what my boss was doing. The complaints went as high as the Governor's office, and at one function, TDCJ's new executive director, Brad Livingston, said to me, 'What do you think of your new boss?' I said, 'I don't think anything of him, he's worthless.' Eventually, Brad hauled him into his office and told him to buck his ideas up, and when he didn't, he was transferred to another department. I was at home, getting dressed, when Brad called and said he needed me in his office at 8.15. I thought I was in trouble, but they made me acting director instead.

I acted as the PIO director for months, without the extra money and anybody helping me, which meant I was on call 24/7. When I went home at 5 p.m., journalists would still be working, so I'd spend my evenings fielding calls. When I became pregnant in 2004, and was at the doctor's office finding out the sex of my child, I was on the phone with a warden, because there was an issue at one of the units. My husband threw a surprise 30th birthday party for me, and I kept having to wander off to answer emails. That's what my life consisted of, it was just a constant dinging and pinging of emails and text messages, mostly mundane media inquiries but also much more significant alerts informing me that a correctional officer had been injured, an inmate had killed himself or someone had tried to escape.

There were one or two attempted escapes every year, and they were exhausting, because they never happened during the day, they would always happen at about 3 a.m. I'd get a call and somebody would say, 'count didn't clear', which meant they'd counted the inmates in a unit and come up short. I'd immediately have to start alerting the media, because it was imperative that the public was notified as soon as possible. If the inmate killed someone, that would have come back on us. In fact, that happened once: an inmate broke into the first house he came to, killed the owner and stole their car, before we could get word out.

If the escape happened in Amarillo, for example, I'd have to look up all the Amarillo media and start sending them information, including a description of the escapee and his mugshot. But it wasn't just about talking to the media, it was about staging the media. You don't want media crawling all over the unit, driving around and filming things they're not supposed to be filming, so I had to get to the unit, find a place to house them and keep updating them, so that they didn't start making stuff up. There was an escape in San Antonio and I had to drive straight there after a board meeting in Austin. I found a Walmart at 3 a.m., bought a pillow and a change of clothes, because it was the middle of summer, and slept in my car.

When we had a hurricane, all the units around the coast would have to be evacuated, which meant I would be in a command centre in Huntsville, handling media alerts while administrators were working out the logistics of moving thousands of inmates to safer ground. It was relentless. After four or five months, they finally gave me the job full-time, and I officially became the first female director of the TDCJ public information office. My first thoughts were, 'Great, can I finally hire some help? And can I also have more money?'

'Good luck dealing w/the media trash and politicians
on "you are killing them like dogs" accusations. Fuck
'em! Btw... saw a great quote, last words of H. Bogart:
"I shouldn't have switched from Scotch to martinis."
Yofitw [Your Only Friend In The World]

Email from Larry to Michelle, 21 March 2004

It was when I became pregnant that witnessing executions ceased to be an abstract concept and became deeply personal. I had read that when a baby was in utero, it can hear, which is why people play music and try to teach them languages. I started to worry that my baby could hear the inmates' last words, their pitiful apologies, their desperate claims of innocence, their spluttering and snoring. I'd have weird, irrational thoughts that an inmate's evil spirit might leave his body and enter my baby's, so that I'd end up giving birth to an evil child. I'd seen it in some Denzel Washington movie, but it still felt real.

Frances Newton, who was on female death row for murdering her husband and two children, including a daughter who was 21 months old, would ask me about my pregnancy all the time. She was always very sweet and polite, but it really made me feel uncomfortable. I'd be thinking, 'You had a baby, and you killed her. Why are you asking about mine?'

I was more fearful in general, terrified of an inmate from the general population punching me in the stomach, which is the kind of thing that can happen to correctional officers at any time, for absolutely no reason. In October 2004, an inmate strangled a female prison clerk to death in a storage closet at the Connally Unit. Because the inmate had a clean disciplinary record, he'd been given janitorial duties, which meant interacting with staff. Once, I was over at the Polunsky Unit, went to the employee restroom, and when I came out of the stall, I suddenly thought, 'What's stopping me from running into an inmate in here?' My thoughts ran the gamut from natural caution to outright paranoia, but even the paranoia was rooted in the realities of my job. I had an operation in 2004, and when they gave me the injection to put me under, I started rambling about executions: 'You don't understand, I watch people die. This is exactly how it happens, and they don't wake up...'

When my daughter was born in March 2005, the doctor picked her up and she didn't make a sound. The silence probably only lasted for about five seconds, but it felt like forever. I was filled with sheer terror, it felt like my whole world was going to collapse. Then she started to cry. After that, the post-execution silence in the death house, when the chemicals had stopped flowing and the doctor was waiting in the wings, became excruciating. I understood that for the inmate's family, that silence lasted forever. From that moment on, I always tried to witness on the victim's side. I said it was because I had to get out first, so I could gather the last statement from the warden's office and hurry to distribute it to the media, but it was mainly because I didn't want to be standing shoulder to shoulder with unfettered grief for any longer than was absolutely necessary.

I had felt empathy for inmates' mothers before, as with Ricky McGinn's, but now I was a mother myself, it was on another level entirely. I just couldn't comprehend how those poor moms could stand there, watching their sons die. I couldn't fathom how they must have been feeling. One inmate told me he didn't want his mom to see him executed, and she'd said, 'I was here when you came into this world, I will be here when you leave it.' I had this little baby at home that I would do anything for, and these women were watching their babies die. Suddenly, executions were things I began to dread.

Very occasionally, motherhood and prison life rubbed up against each other to produce the most beautiful sparks. At the Wynne Unit where I lived in prison housing, there was a gas pump manned by one of the inmates. He was a trustee, which meant he was going home soon, so had no incentive to run. I had a state car assigned to me and I'd sometimes fill up on my way to dropping my child at day care, and that would be the highlight of this inmate's day. I'd roll my window down and he'd say, 'Oh my gosh! What a beautiful baby!' One day when I was driving away, I looked in my rear-view mirror and saw this inmate – a huge, burly man – looking up at the sky and pointing, with this big grin on his face. I reckoned that was him saying, 'God, you're all right...' He was just so happy to have seen my little baby's smile. That was one of the most heart-warming things I ever saw.

But those first couple of executions I witnessed after my daughter was born really messed with my head. I'd arrive at the Walls Unit, see the inmate's family and know immediately who the mom was, because she wouldn't be saying a word. She'd be sitting there, silent and staring, in another world. Whereas before I had to occasionally stifle a tear after an execution, now I'd be weeping all the way home.

I had a cousin who lived in California, which is all about positive vibes, and she advised me to shower as soon as I got home from an execution, to wash away all the bad energy. I took her up on it, but could never wash it away completely. I used to be terrified of lizards: if I saw one in the house, I'd demand someone get rid of it. But now when I saw a little lizard, I'd pick it up and put it outside, because I'd be thinking, 'There might be a momma lizard looking for her baby.'

My beautiful baby at home made my job seem even bleaker and the executions even more ugly. But I still didn't discuss anything with my husband, because I didn't want all that bleakness and ugliness in my home. Was I tougher than those female reporters I used to mock for crying in the bathroom? Nah, I just held it off for longer. I'd become this giant candy-ass, just like them.

CHAPTER 10
A LITTLE BIT DARKER

'Whoever sheds the blood of man, by man shall his blood be shed; for God made man in his own image.'

Genesis 9:6

'All the men and women whom I have faced at that final moment convince me that in what I have done I have not prevented a single murder. Capital punishment, in my view, achieved nothing except revenge.'

Albert Pierrepoint, former British hangman

When I started witnessing executions, I was adamantly pro-death penalty, but I didn't really ask myself what the death penalty was for. It existed in Texas, and I saw it as justice for the victims of the most heinous crimes. That was the long and the short of it. But as time went on, and I got to know the inmates and see how the victims' families reacted to witnessing the person who killed their loved ones die, it became obvious to me that there were no winners. I'd be standing in the witness room thinking, 'There's an inmate over there, dying on a gurney; there's the inmate's family over there, watching him die; there's the victim's family over there, having to listen to the inmate's mother screaming. Everybody is being screwed over, this is all bullshit...'

In most cases, the inmate's family had nothing to do with the crime they committed. They raised their kids as best they could and hoped they'd do right, but, ultimately, they didn't have any control over how they turned out, and they paid a very big price for what their son or father or brother had done. I believe some of the victims' families gained something from executions, at least they said they did. After the execution of Orien Cecil Joiner in 2000, two of his victim's relatives high-fived each other as they left the death chamber. The son of one of Betty Lou Beets' victims raised his fist to the sky in triumph outside the Walls Unit. And after Michael Perry was executed in 2010, his victim's daughter said, 'I needed to look into his eyes and see if he was the monster I had made him out to be. Now I know that he is.' But then there was someone like Linda Purnhagen, whose two children were murdered by Dennis Dowthitt, and who admitted that watching his execution in 2001 'would have been easier if he had been horrible'.

While some family members hoped an execution might bring some sort of closure, others openly admitted that watching an execution brought them no peace. There were even family members who petitioned the Governor to show clemency. The family of Clay Peterson, who was stabbed to death by Johnny Martinez in Corpus Christi in 1993, attempted to get Martinez's sentence commuted to life imprisonment. Jamie Hollis, the nephew of Lonnie Pursley's victim, Robert Cook, wrote Pursley a poem, expressing his forgiveness: 'A soul that is lost, pays no greater cost, than to leave this world, without being forgiven...'

As for Thomas Bartlett Whitaker, his father's ceaseless campaigning for clemency paid off – in February 2018, an hour before he was scheduled to die, Whitaker became the first inmate to be spared by a Texas governor (in this case Greg Abbott) in more than ten years. 'I deserve punishment for my crimes,' said Whitaker, 'but my dad did nothing wrong.'

Family members would often say, more in hope than expectation, that an execution had brought a chapter to an end. But how healthy was it that the chapter had lasted so long? In some cases, inmates were on death row for decades, which is why you heard a lot of family members say, 'Thank God it's finally over with. We can now try to move on and put it behind us.' With the emphasis on 'try'. Robert Lee Powell gunned down a police officer in Austin in 1978, and wasn't executed until 2010. In the time Powell was on death row, 459 inmates were executed. Talk about killing time, and imagine the agony of waiting for the victim's family. Raymond Riles has been on death row since 1976, Harvey Earvin since 1977, and some people question whether an execution loses some of its purpose if it takes place so long after the crime. During his stay on death row, Powell turned from a drug-fuelled killer into a model prisoner, a peacemaker who taught illiterate inmates how to read. His victim's family didn't witness the same man die who killed their loved one.

Some family members were angry that the inmate got to say goodbye to his relatives and tie up loose ends, while their victim or victims weren't afforded that luxury. On the flipside, the inmate and his family had a different type of agony: knowing the exact minute when they should expect death. That's a punishment in itself, and that's presumably why some inmates tried to take their own lives rather than be executed – having that death sentence hanging over them is more than some of them can bear.

Roy Pippin set fire to his cell just before he was due to be taken to the death house in 2007, using a piece of wire stuck in a wall socket, only for the fire to be extinguished by officers. Michael Johnson was more successful. Johnson killed himself 16 hours before his scheduled execution in 2006, by slashing a jugular vein in his arm with a razor blade. He wrote 'I didn't do it' on the wall in blood, although the evidence said otherwise. I wondered if that was because he was terrified of being strapped to the gurney, or it was his way of taking back control, by dying on his own terms, and not the State's.

Some family members left the death chamber angry that the inmate hadn't acknowledged them or apologised. Graczyk would ask them, 'Did his lack of apology bother you?' and the victim's mom or dad might reply, 'Yeah, he's a coward, he should have taken ownership of his crime.' Others said it wouldn't have mattered either way. But these were abstract, hypothetical questions, because nobody really knew what they would have felt had the opposite happened. Others were angry that the inmate had had the audacity to apologise, having not done so previously, while others didn't know how to compute the fact that the inmate had apologised at all. It put them in a dilemma: Did they now have to forgive them? Or was it an eye for an eye? Texas is a very conservative state and goes hand in hand with Christianity, but the Bible can be interpreted in so many different ways. Graczyk would also ask, 'Do you accept the apology he made on the gurney?' Not many did.

For some, the process was rather anti-climactic: they walked into a room and watched the man who killed their loved one go to sleep. There was no blood or gore or screaming, like there would have been when the inmate killed their loved one. I recall one family member saying they would have preferred to see the inmate stoned to death. But mostly it was along the lines of, 'it was over too quickly', or 'he should have felt more pain'.

I agree with Larry, executions don't bring closure, as much as reporters and the wider public demand they do. Executions are generally retribution, pure and simple, although I don't fault the victims' families for wanting retribution, because I'd want it too. I guess the idea is that the victims' families will no longer be tortured by the thought that this evil person is still alive while their loved one is dead. Unfortunately, the grieving never ends.

I came to feel that executions were just sad situations all round. It was sad that a murder had happened and an innocent person lost their life, it was sad that this was what people did to each other, it was sad that we were all standing there watching a man die. What part of that makes anybody feel good? Everybody loses. And I had to witness that sadness over and over again. Being the conduit to the outside world just became so intense and dark. The sadness was winning. As Graczyk also used to ask, 'Are you glad you came?' Who could possibly be glad about anything in such a sad situation?

It began to trouble me that other people couldn't see both sides of the argument. It wasn't my job to present both sides of the argument, but the death penalty was the only hot button topic that I'd had any direct experience of. Whenever I discovered that somebody had a clear position on the death penalty, I'd find myself arguing against it. Somebody would say they were vehemently pro-death penalty, that the state had every right to put a person to death if they'd committed a terrible crime, and I'd find myself saying, 'Okay, I get where you're coming from, but here's the other side of that argument. What about if that person was only 17 when he committed the crime? What if he was no longer a danger to society?'

I was spending more and more time questioning the executions of certain inmates. Leonard Rojas was executed for murdering his girlfriend and brother, whom he suspected of sleeping with each other. I wouldn't have given Rojas the death penalty for that, because it seemed like a crime of passion rather than anything pre-meditated. Then there were the Law of Parties cases, in which the person who pulled the trigger might receive a life sentence, usually after turning in his accomplices and striking a deal, while the person who was known not to have pulled the trigger was sentenced to die. I had a real issue with that, it made no sense to me, there was something maddeningly arbitrary about it.

There would always be someone complaining about last meals – 'I think it's a disgrace that we give them any courtesies after what they did' – and I'd say, 'Have you ever had a relative on death row? No? Well, if you did, would you want them to have a comforting meal before they were executed?' If someone came out as vehemently anti-death penalty, I'd find myself saying, 'But what if your wife was murdered? Do you have a child? What if your daughter was raped and stabbed to death?' I'd back my arguments up with real facts from cases I was familiar with. And by this time, I was familiar with a lot of cases. What if you were the parents of Jennifer Ertman or Elizabeth Peña, who were gang-raped for more than an hour before being stomped to death by Peter Cantu? Would it bother you to see Cantu die? What if you were the parents of Christina Benjamin, who was raped, stabbed, disembowelled and decapitated by Jason Massey in 1993? (On the gurney, Massey finally revealed that he'd thrown Benjamin's head off a bridge, into the Trinity River.) I'd defy people to read the details of some of these cases and not feel sick.

I was arguing all the time, because it bothered me that people held such strong opinions about things they didn't have any experience of. They'd often never known anyone in prison, much less on death row. It wasn't just the death penalty, people being obnoxious about any hot button topic they had no real knowledge of annoyed me. Someone would declare themselves as staunchly anti-abortion, and I'd think, 'Were you faced with a pregnancy when you were 15, having been raped by a psychopathic father?' It got to the point where I was being pretty snarky with one particular reporter, because he was just so right-wing about everything and obnoxiously pro-death penalty. He pissed me off more than most because he was a journalist, so should have seen both sides. I kept making him watch executions from the inmate's side, but even all those mothers weeping and wailing didn't teach him any empathy.

After Larry had left the building for good, I witnessed two executions from the IV room, because I felt I had to. I spent a lot of time talking about executions, but I'd never actually seen the process from start to finish. The warden brought me into the death house at 5.45 p.m., through a narrow pipe chase that runs behind the holding cells, and through this door that leads into the IV room. It was tiny, with a small table, on which were laid the drugs.

When you see pictures of the death chamber, you can see there's a tiny hole in the wall, maybe six inches by six inches, like a little slot, and that's where the IV lines pass through, directly from the needles attached to the inmate. Next to the slot is a one-way glass, and behind that glass is a three- or four-man team, volunteers from the local community with medical training. They can't be actual doctors, because the Hippocratic Oath states that you should 'do no harm'.

From that vantage point, I actually got to see the inmate enter the death chamber, step onto the gurney and get strapped down. It bothered me greatly to witness the inmate's docility. Members of the IV team talked to him while they were swabbing him with alcohol and establishing the lines. It looked like idle chit-chat, and I wondered what they could possibly be saying: 'Hey, how are you?' 'Not great, I'm about to die on a gurney...' But I guess it was similar to giving blood, when the nurse senses you're a bit nervous and says, 'This might pinch.' Then they got the saline solution flowing, the witnesses were brought in and the execution got under way.

There isn't a machine that pushes the syringe, it's done by hand. It's not like a firing squad, where nobody knows who shot the fatal bullet. I saw who administered the drugs, but very few people ever do – as long as I worked there and as many secrets as I knew, even I didn't know who acted as executioner until the day I witnessed from that room. He pushed the syringe to release the first drug, pushed the syringe to release the second and pushed the syringe to release the third. I witnessed from the IV room only twice, because it troubled me so much, seeing the inmate walk unrestrained to the gurney, hopping up there and offering his arms with no hesitation.

I went in for my annual physical and the nurse, who I had known for years, said to me, 'How's work?' I replied that it was fine, and she said, 'You just seem a little bit darker, not your usual bubbly self.' I was used to people seeing me as a happy, smiley person, so that bothered the hell out of me. I'd prided myself on the fact that nobody could notice I was having a hard time and it troubled me that I wasn't as good at hiding it as I thought.

I was always a contradiction, a puzzle to a lot of people. I hold back pieces of myself, because I'm afraid that if anybody sees all of me, they will feel that I shouldn't be loved at all. I am honest and closed, in that I don't tell everything I know. I am breezy and deeply introspective. I didn't want anybody to feel sorry for me, which is why I didn't even tell my husband when I cried all the way home after an execution, because I didn't want him to say, 'You should perhaps go and talk to someone.'

Being seen as strong was so important to me. My mother is a wonderfully strong woman, my grandmothers have been wonderfully strong women, and I didn't want anybody to think I was anything less than they were. But now I'd be in a TDCJ meeting, putting up with all their shit, and find myself tearing up. I've made that particular face an awful lot. If it were a piece of art hanging in a gallery, it would be called 'Determined Through

Tears'. I would be so mad, but more frustrated, because I guarantee my mom or grandma never cried at work about anything.

One of Larry and my favourite things to do was stand outside the Walls Unit and watch inmates be released. The inmates who had done their time and owed nothing else to the state walked out the front door, the inmates who were on parole walked out the side entrance, because they had to tie things up with the parole office. They'd all come out in a big swarm, carrying these little red onion sacks, in which would be their belongings.

It was the coolest thing to watch a former inmate break into a huge smile and see their kids running up the street, before jumping into their arms. Or you'd see a former inmate tenderly embracing and kissing his wife or girlfriend. That gave me chills. But more and more I just felt sad for those former inmates who had nobody to greet them and were having to watch all this joy around them. You'd see them trudge off towards the Greyhound station with their bus voucher in one hand and onion sack over their shoulder. Who knew where they were going, whether they had anybody to go to or whether they'd soon be back.

In October 2007, a fisherman in Galveston Bay found the body of a little girl, stuffed into a plastic container. Her injuries meant she was unrecognisable, and the media dubbed her 'Baby Grace'. The following month, police arrested Kimberly Ann Trenor and her husband Royce Clyde Zeigler, out of Spring, Texas. The girl's name was Riley Ann Sawyers, and Trenor was her mother and Zeigler her stepfather. When Trenor was questioned by police, she confessed that she and Zeigler had beaten the little girl with leather straps and held her head underwater in a bath tub, before Zeigler had picked her up by her hair and thrown her across the room, causing her head to smash against the floor. The couple hid her remains in a shed for two months before throwing her off a bridge.

My daughter was about the same age as Riley Ann, and they both had this really fine, blonde hair. So I couldn't get this image out of my head, of Riley Ann being swung around by her hair. I'd be reading about it in my office and weeping. I read the same article over and over again. It was just so horrible, but I couldn't not read it. That case really tore me up. This woman, who was originally from Ohio, had fled with the baby to another state, so that the baby's biological father was fraught with worry, and then she'd let this asshole she was married to beat her child to death. That was one of the few times I rooted for somebody to be executed.

It always bugged me that women weren't treated the same as men when it came to the death penalty. Women committed some of the most detestable crimes in Texas, often crimes against their own children, and didn't get executed. There was a case out of Beaumont, where a former correctional officer named Kenisha Berry killed one of her children and attempted to kill another. She put duct tape over her four-day-old son's mouth, threw him in a trash bag and tossed him in a dumpster, while he was still alive. A few years later, another newborn baby was found abandoned in a ditch, covered in fire-ant bites, but she survived. Berry was sentenced to death, but that decision was later overturned, because it was decided the prosecution had not adequately proved that she was a continuing threat to society, only to her own children. It seemed like women wanted equality, except when it came to the death penalty.

My best friend worked at the District Attorney's office in Galveston, and I asked her if they were going to push for the death penalty for Trenor. She said no, and I was so upset. I just couldn't understand why not. Prosecutors decided it was unlikely the jury would have sentenced her to death. I thought that was bullshit. All these irrational thoughts started swirling in my head. I wondered if I could somehow get to this woman. I worked for the prison system, there had to be a way. It's not as if I was hatching a plan with pen and paper, they were just thoughts, but wild all the same. I felt so strongly that justice wouldn't be done.

I was right. In 2009, Trenor was sentenced to life in prison, with the possibility of parole after 38 years. The jurors wept. Zeigler got life without parole. The state didn't seek the death penalty for him, either. While she was awaiting trial, Trenor gave birth again.

It took a long time for me to start unravelling, but now it had begun. In 2008, when my daughter was three, I got divorced. My husband is a good man, and a great dad, but we just weren't compatible. It had nothing to do with anxieties over my job, it's just that the opposites attract thing hadn't lasted too long. I'm not regretful at all, we had a beautiful daughter together that I wouldn't have had otherwise, and I thank God for her every day.

CHAPTER 11
STEALING TIME

'The [TDCJ] admin suffers from intellectual incest. They all live in a little town, went to the same little college in Huntsville and are terrified of new ideas. I've never worked in a stranger place.'

John Hurt, former TDCJ spokesperson

'The core values of the Texas Department of Criminal Justice are Courage, Perseverance, Integrity and Commitment.'

From the TDCJ website

Under executive director Brad Livingston, TDCJ became increasingly opaque and fearful. For years, everything I learned from Larry I applied to my role, but that transparent way of doing things went out of fashion. People called Brad 'The Bean Counter', because he had been TDCJ's chief financial officer. People also used to wonder why he was running a prison system, because he had never worked in corrections.

Whereas previous directors left us alone to do what we had to do, Brad's motto was 'no news is good news', which meant he often made it difficult for me to do my job. He didn't understand how to handle the media, because he didn't have any kind of background in journalism, and he wasn't interested in my advice either. That said, the suspicion was that Livingston and his deputy Bryan Collier were taking most of their cues from Houston Senator John Whitmire.

When Lawrence Brewer was scheduled to die in 2011, for his part in the Jasper dragging case 13 years earlier, he ordered a last meal that would have fed 10 men. Inmates usually ordered their last meals two weeks before their execution date, but on the day of the execution, some would find themselves too nervous to eat any of it. That's what happened with Brewer. When the warden asked him if he wanted his last meal, Brewer replied, 'You know what? I don't think I'm gonna be able to eat.' The warden said he'd bring in a few snacks anyway, in case he changed his mind, and that was it. The following day, Whitmire read about Brewer's last meal request and went ballistic. He was angry that Brewer had ordered all this food and not eaten it, thinking it was Brewer taking one last jab at the prison system and his victims. That simply wasn't the case – it was clear to everyone who was there that Brewer was just nervous. What Whitmire also didn't seem to appreciate was that a last meal request is exactly that, a request. A condemned man could request what he liked, that didn't mean he was going to get it, just as Odell Barnes didn't get justice, equality and world peace.

Whitmire claimed to be outraged that this evil man was being shown compassion and demanded that the prison system do away with last meals. Previous executive directors of TDCJ would have told Whitmire that they appreciated his concern, but that they were going to continue serving last meals anyway. But Livingston immediately caved. That day after Brewer's execution, last meals were scrapped, and from that time on, condemned men ate whatever their fellow inmates happened to be eating. If the units were on lockdown, which happened several times a year so that officers could search for contraband, the condemned man might get a peanut butter sandwich and an apple, because the inmates who would normally be working in the kitchen were locked in their cells.

I viewed last meals as respect for a prisoner's humanity, the right thing to do. Yes, Brewer had committed a horrible crime, but this was a tradition dating back decades, and there were certainly other inmates who asked for larger, more elaborate and more ridiculous last meals. Because of an uninformed, knee-jerk reaction by a lawmaker who had no knowledge of what Brewer actually received, and because none of our administrators thought to ask those of us who had actually been there, we were doing away with last meals, so that the condemned couldn't even look forward to a cheeseburger before they died on the gurney.

I don't know what Charles Reynolds got to eat before he was led to the electric chair in 1924, but it wouldn't surprise me if it was more comforting than a crappy sandwich and a piece of fruit. But I was more upset about what Livingston's capitulation represented. It showed that the agency was feeble and at the mercy of people who didn't understand anything about the prison system.

I sometimes wondered how Larry would have coped under the new leadership. I suspect they would have had far less tolerance, because they were so anti-media and TDCJ was no longer a place for mavericks. Because I was still young and malleable, I went along with it for a while. But some of it was difficult to stomach.

TDCJ became more and more paranoid about what we could release to the public, and I started arguing with them regularly, not just the directors but also the office's general counsel. The Texas

Open Records Act required us to hand over existing information immediately on request, but they started ignoring this provision, instead waiting until the eleventh hour to release information that we had readily available. I wondered why they were suddenly playing this game. Members of the media were asking for something we had, so why weren't we just turning it over? I'd be told it wasn't public information, and I'd say, 'But almost everything we have is public information!' Access also became a problem. A reputable TV crew out of San Antonio wanted to film the death chamber in HD, but Livingston told me not to let them in. I fought and fought and that just made him angry, because it looked like I wasn't on his side. I wasn't enough of a yes woman, and butting heads with authority started to wear on me.

There was a prison unit in Sugar Land, which is a fast-growing suburb of Houston. The Central Unit sat on acreage now worth millions of dollars, and the City of Sugar Land wanted to build an airport extension on it. It wasn't a secret, they even had a scale model of the extension in the existing airport. They lobbied the Texas Legislature to close the unit and finally the Legislature agreed, directing TDCJ to shut up shop in 2011. When the media asked why it was being shuttered, I explained that the land had become very valuable and the City of Sugar Land wanted an airport extension, having successfully lobbied the Legislature for rights to the land. Whitmire went nuts, calling Bryan Collier to demand that I be directed to stop telling the media the truth, replacing it with a narrative favourable to him.

Specifically, I was instructed to tell the media that we were closing that unit because of prison reforms Whitmire had passed, which reduced the prison population and made the unit unnecessary. I guess in this narrative, the City of Sugar Land's successful lobby for the unit was just a coincidence. I thought, 'Okay, the population has gone down, which is why we are able to absorb the Central Unit inmates at other state lockups, but that's not why that unit is being closed. There are plenty of other units in various states of disrepair that would have been closed before that one.' Whitmire's version of events wasn't true, so I refused to parrot it. The reporters liked me because I was honest and gave them accurate information, just like Larry, and I wasn't going to stake my reputation on a big lie. I talked around the issue, said stuff like 'there are a number of issues at play'. It all went downhill from there.

'Some flacks [public information officers] live to circle the wagons and block the free flow of public information. But Lyons works her ass off to make sure that if a reporter's going to write something about an institution as massive and complex as TDCJ, that reporter's going to have the correct information, and they're going to have it ASAP. She's fast, patient, whip-smart and doesn't make you feel like an idiot for asking possibly stupid questions. She gets the job done.'

Houston Press, announcing Michelle as 'best flack' 2009

In November 2011, I was told I was under investigation for falsifying my timesheets. My bosses at TDCJ said I'd been claiming for hours spent in the office when I wasn't there. But Larry had hired me as an exempt employee, which in the US means you work a certain number of hours a week and receive a set salary, even if you've done a ton of overtime. On the day of an execution, or when there was a prison escape, I might work 14 hours, but maybe leave early the following day. But now they made me go back through my timesheets and if, for example, there was a day when I'd left 15 minutes early, they ruled that I had to take those 15 minutes as vacation. When I protested that what they were doing was against the law because of my status as an exempt employee, they went ahead with a hearing anyway, without showing me the results of their investigation. I was found guilty, suspended for five days, put on probation and demoted. They didn't want to get rid of me completely, because although my code of transparency made people uncomfortable, they were also aware I was good at my job and popular among the reporters.

Usually when they wanted someone out, they'd make up an irrelevant position elsewhere, but keep them on at the same salary and hope they resigned in time. But I was now doing the same job for $12,000 less. Why was I the only one who got a pay cut? I met with a lawyer friend in Huntsville and he helped me file an Open Records Request. Aside from asking for all the documents from my investigation, I asked for specific records that only I knew existed.

I knew they were talking about me via their BlackBerries, because they had something called PIN-to-PIN, which meant the messages weren't stored anywhere. I got hold of one of the messages by accident, because it was part of a forwarded email chain, but they refused to turn any more over, which is a violation of the Open Records Act.

I met with Bryan Collier, the short-statured deputy executive director who did all of Brad Livingston's dirty work. Collier's words to me were, 'I should have just fired you.' I said, 'Well, you didn't, and now we're here.' They banished me to a different office, which was infested with flying cockroaches and bees. I sat there for hours on end, vigilantly watching for honey-covered roaches that might fly down from the ceiling, while twiddling my thumbs, because they were no longer sending calls my way.

I knew my career in the prison system was over, but they still wanted me to watch men die. I liked George Rivas a lot, and I didn't want to go in that room and see him be executed. Was he a good person? Not really, he killed a cop. Should I have liked him? Probably not. But I'd gotten to know him over the years and he was smart and engaging. Then again, they could have been executing the Devil and I wouldn't have wanted to see it. Walking up the steps of the Walls Unit, my shoes felt like they had lead in them. I must have looked like a condemned man, dragging his feet on his way to the gurney.

Ten years earlier, I probably would have commented in my journal that Rivas looked like somebody I knew, written up my story and gone out for margaritas. But my shield wasn't as strong as it had been, and I cried in my car instead.

I was banned from board meetings and legislative hearings after Whitmire accused me of looking uninterested and snapping gum. He later admitted he'd mistaken me for somebody else, after a reporter informed him I wasn't actually present at that meeting. At times, the bullying and harassment was farcical, like a bungled hit.

One day, I moved some press releases I'd written from a shared folder to a private folder, because I wasn't going to allow Jason Clark, my former subordinate who was now trying to take my job, to also take my work. I figured that if we were now doing the same job at the same pay, he could write his own press releases. The moment he noticed he no longer had unfettered access to my work, he tattled to Bryan Collier, who called me into another disciplinary meeting, during which my computer was confiscated. I ended up with another charge, this one for 'misconduct'. An administrator assigned to conduct one of my investigations said to me, 'This is one of the most ridiculous things I've ever had to do', but I was still found guilty, because the bosses had already decided on the punishment.

I decided it was time to remove my belongings from my old office, so I visited after-hours, taking with me everything I had amassed during my time at TDCJ – books, inmate art and all my execution files, including the notes I'd taken since my days at *The Huntsville Item*. The following day, Collier called me, said that all my files now belonged to him and demanded I return them. When

I told him that I'd be keeping them, because many of the files were from my time as a reporter, contained public information and my own notes, he threatened to call the police and have me charged with theft. I replied, 'Do what you gotta do', and hung up on him. I then put a call in to TDCJ's Inspector General and explained the situation. He told me that Collier was within his rights to insist I hand the files back, but brokered a deal for me to return them much later in the day. I made copies of every single note I ever took, and those documents form the spine of this book.

After having my computer confiscated, I was moved to a different division completely, where my role was to field research enquiries from students and academics. I told my new boss in advance, 'Everything I do from this point on has nothing to do with anything you've done. I'm just doing what I have to do.' She understood. In my new role, I'd get calls from women who weren't able to visit their sons or husbands because they were imprisoned in units many miles away. Because I still knew a lot of people in the prison system, I pulled some strings and got some of the inmates moved. It was not official, but nobody ever found out.

TDCJ's expectation was that if a reporter contacted me, I was to ignore them. That wasn't going to happen. These were people I'd built up relationships with for 11 years, so I wasn't going to act like they suddenly didn't exist. I'd tell them to contact Jason Clark, the guy I hired who was now in my job. That was a bitter pill to swallow. The final straw was when I received an email from a blogger, who was a correctional officer at one of our units. I'd always been told not to reply to this guy, because they didn't consider him to be a journalist. My view was that this was the internet age, he was one of ours, and I worked for the public information office, therefore I should help him with any information he requested. In his email, the blogger complained that I hadn't replied to a previous request, and copied Whitmire in on it. I replied, leaving Whitmire copied in, and filled him in on everything that had happened to me. Within an hour, my computer access had been terminated and I was written up for insubordination.

My crime this time was communicating with a journalist, when I'd been told not to. I did point out that they'd previously told me they didn't consider him to be a journalist, but by now they were just fucking with me. When I spoke to a woman from HR, she said, 'You know what's gonna happen tomorrow.' I knew that meant they were planning to fire me. I realised I was going to have to get another job immediately, and that it would look better if I quit. I drafted a resignation letter, waited until my new boss left for the day and slid it under her door. With that, I was gone.

'Michelle Lyons was the last line of defense and the open door that provided some sense of transparency for an agency still living and operating in the dark ages. With her gone, the agency will surely suffer a huge blow to their ability to be believable and honest.'

The Backgate Website, 10 May 2012

There were only a handful of people in TDCJ I had no respect for, but nobody wanted to put a target on their back and make a stand on my behalf. I was close to a woman who worked in the Governor's office and said to her, 'Please, you can stop this?' But she didn't want to get involved. TDCJ employees I thought I was friends with didn't want to know either, including some who de-friended or blocked me on Facebook.

What TDCJ did to me broke my heart – it was the worst thing that had ever happened to me. Family members and close friends die, relationships end, and all those things are awful. But this was a different kind of grief.

I'd tried so hard to do everything that Larry had taught me, and watching all those executions had taken a toll. I took so many hits for TDCJ. When Whitmire was upset and on the warpath, I'd tell Livingston that I'd put out a press release and make any quotes attributable to me, so that Whitmire wouldn't get angry with him. One time, Livingston said to me, 'I don't know how you do what you do, I could never watch an execution.' But he didn't have any qualms about sending me in there, over and over again, without ever asking if I was coping. That's how cheap I was to him. Livingston didn't even have the nuts to sit down with me and tell me what was going on. Instead, he got his lapdog Collier to handle it all, drum up this bullshit stuff and paint me as this shady person who was rigging my timesheets. I'd been hired by Larry to ensure transparency, had spent years being as helpful as I possibly could to reporters, and now I was being punished for doing the very same thing.

You know what they told me at my initial investigation? That I'd been 'stealing the state's time'. Are you fucking kidding me? They stole plenty of time from me – hours working on escapes and executions and every other crisis – but more than anything, they stole my peace of mind. All I stole from them was a stapler when I left. And, no, they're not getting that fucking stapler back, even if they beg for it.

I'd started working while I was still at college, so I'd never had a hiatus. I'd never back-packed around Europe or taken a career break, all I'd ever done as an adult was work. So now I didn't know what to do with my time. And how do you enjoy it when you're feeling heartbroken and depressed? I'd remarried in 2011, but I was the main breadwinner and trying to figure out how to make enough money to hang on to my house and my car and pay my bills. My husband and family were angry at the prison system, and it was nice to have their support, but there was nothing they could do. It was summer 2012 when I left, and I'd lay by the pool with my daughter, crying behind my sunglasses. I was mentally shattered.

I'd always had the ability to bounce back quickly from a knock. I am a very confident person by nature, but this was the exception. It felt like the things that came so easily to other people were beyond my grasp, that I couldn't get things to line up or the pieces to fit. My head was swimming. All I wanted to do was fold in on myself and be left alone, while at the same time wanting people to realise I needed a life vest. I'd tied so much of my identity up with that job, and if I was no longer the spokesperson for the prison system, what was I? And maybe I wasn't as good as I thought I was? I didn't know where to go or what to do, and that just wasn't me.

I was getting blackballed from other state agencies, and it's not like a lot of places had a real need for a specialist in crisis communications. I'd spent the previous 11 years telling people about the nuts and bolts of the prison system, about things that didn't happen anywhere else: riots in Mineral Wells; escapees stealing a truck and killing an officer on horseback in Huntsville; a sex offender pulling a gun on his guards while passing through Conroe; a death row inmate with 25 bottles of hooch hidden in his cell; the guy who kept a pet mouse in a matchbox; countless suicide attempts in units all over the state, some successful, most not; outbreaks of mumps and flu and pretty much everything else; inmates smearing themselves with their own faeces; inmates throwing urine and semen in officers' faces; inmates with cell phones hidden up their asses; inmates trying to milk black widows for their venom… for God's sake! It was a very specific thing that I did, a niche market. You don't tend to find many people with cell phones up their asses in the free world, and if you know of anybody trying to milk black widows for their venom, you should probably let somebody know. My situation reminded me of that line from a song by Jimmy Buffett: 'After all the years I've found my occupational hazard being my occupation's just not around'.

My biggest hang-up was that nobody would remember I'd ever existed. It was a similar feeling to being dumped by my first boyfriend, only ten times worse. With a break-up, you're sad and confused, but when I divorced my first husband, I was reasonably certain I wasn't going to die alone. But when I left TDCJ, all I could think was, 'I'm never gonna have a job that I care about again. Never. Again. For the rest of my days.' I'd lost all that time with my family, watched all these people die, gone through so much shit, and I was now convinced the reporters and rank and file staff at TDCJ would forget about me as soon as I walked out of the door for the last time. I thought I was destined to be that lonely gravestone, overgrown with weeds, that nobody ever visits.

My husband assured me that wasn't going to happen, and he was right. A lot of journalists I'd worked with for all those years covered my story, which I appreciated. I'd tried my best to treat them well, and they paid me back when I really needed it. I still got calls all the time, from reporters telling me Jason Clark wasn't helping them. It made me feel good – maybe I wasn't as suck-ass as I thought I was?

TDCJ's new spokesperson John Hurt called and confided that he was having real problems. He couldn't get his head around the environment, couldn't understand why they insisted on replying to reporters by email, which journalists hate. He was confounded by the agency's lack of transparency, the fact they actively dissuaded him to talk to the media and became 'unglued' when he did. And when he came out and criticised the agency in public, I felt vindicated. Now people knew I wasn't just a bitter ex-employee, because here was a man with years of experience, a veteran of the Texas Department of Transportation, also saying that TDCJ had serious problems. When I read that line about TDCJ being 'intellectually incestuous', I laughed out loud; I thought that was the best.

There were some really good administrators and leaders in the prison system who I respected immensely, but there were others who had no business being there, including Livingston and Collier. Huntsville is a small town, and a lot of TDCJ leaders had known each other for decades. They went to school together at Sam Houston State, studying criminal justice; they were correctional officers together; they came through the ranks together, because they were constantly promoting one another. It was an old-boy system, and old pals tend to stick together. They become stale, because they aren't interested in anything or anyone from outside their network. They become insular, protective and fearful.

Fighting an organisation as huge as TDCJ is unpleasant and intimidating and not for the weak, but I couldn't not do it. One of Livingston's favourite sayings was, 'It's a marathon, not a sprint.' And now I made it mine. They'd won all the early battles, but I was determined to win the war. I'd been so loyal to those people and they had betrayed me. I knew I was on the side of right, and I couldn't let them get away with it. There was a principle at stake.

My attorney was recommended by a reporter-turned-friend from the *Houston Chronicle*, a very good, relentless journalist who was pissed when she found out what was happening to me. While my attorney prepared the case, the central plank of which was that I was a victim of gender discrimination, I started work at the Israeli Consulate in Houston. I was disgraced and in the process of suing my former employer, so I didn't think anyone would want to touch me with a ten-foot pole. But the Israelis didn't care about any of that, which is why I feel so warmly towards them. I was Humpty Dumpty, who had fallen off a wall and shattered into a million pieces, but they picked me up and helped put me back together again. Very quickly, it felt like I was part of this big, loud, funny family that I loved dearly.

Life was still tough. I was making half of what I had at TDCJ, so I had to trade in my car, a big SUV, because I couldn't afford the gas. I probably would have lost my house, but received an $8,000 cheque for backdated unemployment in the nick of time. Then, in August 2013, a federal court judge in Houston, who was always going to side with the prison system, tossed my lawsuit. At that point, you can either quit or you can take your case to the federal court of appeals. So we dusted ourselves off and went back to war, filing an appeal with the US Fifth Circuit Court of Appeals in New Orleans.

I had to live it for more than two years, repeating my story over and over again, including an eight-hour deposition with our opposition, the Texas Attorney General's office, with four or five people sitting across the table from me and my lawyer. I even drove to Austin just to listen to Jason Clark's deposition, because I thought, 'You know what? If you're gonna lie, you're gonna lie to my face.' I stared at him the whole time, to make him as uncomfortable as possible, and every time he said something, I'd ostentatiously write in my notebook and whisper something to my lawyer. We just wanted to shake the little weasel up a bit, and by the look on his face, it seemed to do the trick.

They expected me to fold and walk away, but the whole sorry saga taught me that I was a lot tougher than I thought I was. I spent a lot of time thinking, 'I worked for TDCJ for 11 years, but did they ever pay attention to who I was? Did they really think I was going to lie down and roll over? This could not have been a surprise to them.' The whole time, I was getting emails and calls from TDCJ employees, telling me they were going through something similar and wondering how to fight it. Now it felt like I was fighting for them as well.

The court of appeals said that it was improper that Larry's affidavit, which confirmed that I'd filled out my timesheets exactly as he'd told me, was not introduced by the original judge. The court also agreed that Jason Clark had been filling out his timesheets the same as me, and as such I had been discriminated against. Jason got promoted, while I ended up heartbroken and depressed and crying by the pool. The Attorney General's Office must have advised TDCJ to stop fighting and wasting taxpayer money on the case, because they agreed to a financial settlement. I'd won, and it felt wonderful.

At the settlement conference, the lawyer for the Attorney General's office told me that it should never have gotten this far, I'd been done wrong, and they'd heard it was because I'd had a disagreement with a senator in Houston. But once we'd agreed an amount and TDCJ had paid me out, now it was my time. I thought, 'Go ahead and let it all out.' If a reporter or blogger wanted to know what had happened, I told them, in gory detail, because it was clear that certain publications were on my side. I called for Livingston and Collier to be sanctioned, I said that Jason Clark should be investigated for perjury, having lied about his timekeeping practices under oath in his deposition, and warned journalists to be wary of any information he dispensed to them. I knew from my time at TDCJ that they'd just have to take the criticism, which I enjoyed immensely.

TDCJ released a statement saying my case was 'without merit'. But the appeal court's ruling was there in black and white. I didn't care if people thought I was bitter. I was bitter, I hated those lying assholes. But the tax-paying public also had a right to know, because it was their money TDCJ were forced to pay me. A few years later, a judge friend of mine, with contacts at the Office of Inspector General, told me that TDCJ had indeed fabricated the whole case against me, to keep Senator Whitmire sweet. I also discovered that Jason Clark was earning $21,000 more than me for doing the same job. Had we known that at the time, we could have taken TDCJ to the cleaners.

'Hey, here's a phrase to make your day go by a lot smoother: "Happiness isn't getting what you want, it's wanting what you got!"'

Letter from Randy Arroyo to Michelle, 17 July 2002. Arroyo's sentence was commuted to life in 2005

CHAPTER 12
BURSTING OPEN

'I am a servant of the public... and the public, through its representatives on the press, ought to have some assurance that the details of each execution are carried out decently and in order.'

James Berry, former British hangman, 1892

'It was a creepy, furtive, and shameful affair, in which the participants could not decently show their faces or quite meet one another's eye... I am clear on one thing. Death requires no advocates. It is superfluous to volunteer for its service.'

Christopher Hitchens, 'Scenes from an Execution', 1998

Losing my job at TDCJ was the worst break-up I ever went through. But if they hadn't forced me out, I'd probably still be there, tied up in this dysfunctional relationship. And how many executions would I have seen now? 340? 350? I'd still be telling myself that this was my life's vocation, what I was put on earth to do: watch people die on a gurney.

When I was going through all those disciplinaries at TDCJ, when I was demoted and thought I was going to be fired, I'd pray for it all to stop. I'd think, 'Well, apparently God hates me. Why would He let this happen otherwise? He knows these people are doing me wrong, He knows these people are lying, so why is He doing nothing to stop it?' But sometimes God tries to push you in a direction you refuse to go in, by making things as shitty as possible.

It had to happen the way it did, because I was too scared, stubborn and loyal to leave of my own volition. I'd become institutionalised, no different to some of the inmates. In hindsight, it would be wrong to say I was comfortable, but I was set in my ways. I didn't want to be released, because life on the outside seemed so alien and scary.

My execution journal from years earlier tells me that things were never neat, and they got messier and messier as time went on. But although there were all these threads that were itching away at me, I didn't expect them to add up to this big patchwork quilt that would eventually start suffocating me. So as much as it peeves me to say it, TDCJ did me a favour. I still think about the injustice sometimes, because I did this really tough job that had an impact on me I will never be able to escape or wash my hands of, and these people tried to destroy my reputation and received no punishment.

For a while after I left the prison system, I wondered if I was partly to blame for how it all ended. Maybe I should have kept my mouth shut? Maybe I should have toed the line? But eventually I thought, 'Fuck that. That's not who I am. They were doing me wrong and I stood up for myself', and the bitterness eventually began to subside. Like Robert Coulson once told me, 'you bring sunshine to death row'. Maybe that was my role, to make things better for some of those inmates and move on.

I miss what the job was when I first took it; I miss Fitzgerald; I miss working with the media; I miss visiting the units; I miss interacting with the correctional officers, the wardens and even the inmates. I do not miss executions in any way.

Some people thought I deserved what I got, because they saw me as part of this machinery of killing. Some of the comments were scathing, but they didn't bother me. I read a letter in *The Huntsville Item*, in which someone called me 'the puppet of TDCJ'. I thought, 'Well, yeah, that might not be the most flattering depiction, but I was kind of paid to be their puppet.' But most people were more sympathetic and saw me as somebody who had worked for the company in a company town, with not a lot of other opportunities. It turned out that I had more opportunities than I thought, I just didn't see them at the time. Besides, I never thought I was doing anything wrong. I didn't lie, but neither did I tell everything I knew. It was just my job to be TDCJ's mouthpiece. And the longer I was out of the prison system, the more I realised I'd done my job well.

I kept in touch with Larry, who never sent me a Christmas or birthday card, but did get in contact on St Patrick's Day, Dorothy Parker's birthday and the date that Prohibition was repealed. And I don't think there's a single reporter I haven't kept in contact with, whether from Texas or further afield. Some of them enjoy sharing the little problems they have with the TDCJ public information office, in its current, opaque form. Five years after I left, new reporters are told to seek me out, by their predecessors and even inmates, so I can help them get the real story, because the guy who replaced me, who is earning 21 grand more than I did, isn't helping.

Most of these crime reporters are sharp as razors. Larry always used to say to me, 'If Mike Ward from the *Austin American-Statesman* calls and asks you a question, he already knows the answer. If he asks about a new policy and you say it doesn't exist, he'll pull the policy out of his ass. So never try to be dishonest with him.' But the new breed were terrified of saying something wrong, so they started saying nothing instead. Now, you'll often see the line in articles: 'A TDCJ spokesperson said in an email.' That's their little jab at the system, them telling their readers: 'Hey, I tried to get them to talk to me, but they didn't want to.'

TDCJ has also passed a rule whereby they no longer let reporters from outside the community where the crime took place witness executions. When I started out at TDCJ, there would be a waiting list, reporters from all over Texas would be scrapping for a spot in the witness rooms. Towards the end, budget constraints meant newspapers weren't sending local reporters and were relying on Graczyk's story for the Associated Press instead. There were even a few occasions when *The Huntsville Item* blew off an execution, which pissed me off. A person was being executed in their town and they didn't think it was important enough to cover? What could possibly be happening in Huntsville that day that was more important than someone being executed? But now, even if you wanted to witness, they might not let you. One journalist told me they applied to witness, only to be accused of having 'a morbid curiosity'. They wouldn't even let him into any of the prisons. The guy was writing a book about the death penalty and asking for guidance, but TDCJ wasn't interested in helping. That goes against everything Larry taught me, which is why it is so upsetting.

We felt it was important to have all of those spots filled in the witness rooms and not to build walls, because we didn't have anything to hide. We held back things we needed to, but we genuinely tried to be helpful. TDCJ is a state-funded entity, carrying out a death sentence handed down by a state district court, yet they don't seem to think the people have a right to know what's going on in their death chamber. As Paul Watler, a board member of the Freedom of Information Foundation of Texas, put it, 'It does not serve the public interest and is certainly not transparent to have seats for the news media that are not utilized because the department will not permit, in some cases, accredited news organizations to attend.'

TDCJ's decision to restrict witness spots came on the back of botched executions in Ohio, Oklahoma and Arizona in 2014. In Oklahoma, an inmate named Clayton Lockett was injected with an untested mixture of drugs and took about 45 minutes to die on the gurney. It was determined he died of a heart attack rather than the chemicals, which is undoubtedly a cruel and unusual way to die, no better than burning up in the electric chair or being left hanging and still breathing on the scaffold. In Ohio, Dennis McGuire was convulsing on the gurney for 25 minutes before he finally expired. In Arizona, Joseph Wood was said to be gulping for air for almost two hours before finally being put out of his misery. All three states were using a new cocktail of drugs because companies, whose pharmacies were often based in Europe, either decided to stop manufacturing the drugs or selling them to states with the death penalty.

Texas switched from a three-drug protocol to a one-drug protocol in 2012. From whom or where Texas was buying its drugs was anybody's guess, because TDCJ was allowed to keep it a secret. TDCJ claimed that revealing its suppliers would put those companies at risk of retaliation, which is bullshit. Why shouldn't people know? Tax dollars pay for those drugs, which are being used to execute people. The public needs to know those drugs are coming from a safe place, and it's absurd that TDCJ has fought that. I suspect the real reason they're not telling people is that if they did, the companies would stop selling the drugs for the sake of their reputations, and then Texas wouldn't be able to execute anybody.

After I left, I didn't pay much attention to executions and never had the sense I was missing a game. I was like most people in Huntsville, unaware they were happening on my doorstep. I'd occasionally get calls from reporters, who wanted my knowledge as a prison expert, although I'd usually turn them down if they were from Europe, because they were only going to twist things.

In December 2012, I left the Israeli Consulate after landing a public relations job at a law firm in Houston. I gained petty satisfaction from the fact I was now earning more money than I had at TDCJ, and it was a blessed relief not to be disseminating bad news about hostage situations or suicides or prison 'disturbances'.

My daughter knew I'd worked for the prison system and understood the concept of inmates from a young age. She would see them in their white outfits, picking up trash on the streets of Huntsville, and say, 'Mama, those are the bad men.' And I'd say,

'No, they did a bad thing or got lost in life, that doesn't necessarily make them bad.' I thought it was important to make that distinction.

I was watching a piece on TV about Anthony Graves, who was convicted of murdering a family of six in 1992 and spent 12 years on death row, before being exonerated and freed in 2010. My daughter asked me what 'execution' meant, and I tried to explain. But I didn't want to tell her I had been in that room when they died and that I knew that room so well. When she was about ten, a TV crew came down from Houston to interview me and I let her sit in on that. She would have figured it out eventually, so I wanted to beat people to the punch, any kids or parents who might have said, 'Your mom used to watch people die for a living.' She's an easy-going kid and feels the same way about me as I feel about my mom. I'm her rock, and as long as I'm there for her, she doesn't ask many questions about why I did the things I've done.

It was during the long commutes from my home in Huntsville to my office in Houston that the zipper finally jammed and my mental suitcase burst open. Whenever things happen to me that don't make sense, I go numb, before eventually coming out of it and sorting through things. I had to try to make sense of all these thoughts that were flooding me or I was never going to escape them, and those long drives gave me an awful lot of time to think. Out of nowhere, I'd see the unknown inmate on the gurney, with one tear rolling down his face, or the wrinkled hands of Ricky McGinn's mother pressed against the glass. Whenever I saw those hands, they made me cry. Imagine watching your child die in front of you and not being able to do anything to stop it. Then I might remember one of the mothers from a victim's press conference, sitting silently, almost in a daze, while her husband fielded questions about what it was like to witness the execution of their daughter's murderer. And again, that fear would rise within me, because the worst thing you can imagine had actually happened to them.

One morning in 2013, having just dropped my daughter off at school, I called Larry. We got to talking about our time together at TDCJ, and I suddenly felt compelled to ask if he ever thought about the executions he'd witnessed. I'd never had that conversation with Larry before, it wasn't a road I was prepared to go down. I'd wanted him to think it was no big deal, just like I'd wanted everyone to think it was no big deal. I was a tough chick, and watching men die was just something I did to make a living, so when people asked me about it, I'd tell them the funny parts and leave out the rest. But now I'd thrown it out there, Larry told me that he had nightmares about the executions all the time.

I only ever had one dream about an execution. In it, my grandma was being executed, for murdering her husband. I was really close to my mom's mom, and named my daughter after her. But in the dream, even though it was my grandma on the gurney, I kept telling myself I couldn't cry, because I had a job to do. When I told my grandma, she thought it was the funniest thing ever. So it surprised me that Larry was having these nightmares, because he had been gone for so long. I thought, 'God, for ten years he's been having these bad dreams – is the same thing gonna happen to me?'

It was scary, because Larry seemed like such a strong person. In my mind, he had never stopped being that badass who impressed me so much as a young reporter, the hard-nosed, wise-cracking public information guy from central casting. At the same time, I'd always assumed Larry was anti-death penalty, and would therefore have more trouble than me dealing with what he'd seen. I used to tease him, call him a 'fucking hippy', because he was this liberal guy out of Austin. But now he told me he wasn't as anti-death penalty as I thought he was, which bothered me, because it suggested I had plenty of nightmares of my own to look forward to. But mostly I felt sad that he was still struggling, and bad that I hadn't realised.

Larry Fitzgerald

When TDCJ offered me that retirement package, I just thought, 'I'm out of here, man.' I was ready to go. But shortly after leaving, I got a call out of the blue from a lawyer I knew from my time at the State Bar of Texas. The next thing I knew, I had all these attorneys sitting around my kitchen table, asking me about my relationship with a death row inmate named Thomas Miller-El: what kind of guy was he, how did he spend his time in prison, what did you speak to him about? Thomas committed a horrible crime in Irving in 1985 when he and his wife held up a motel, shot a clerk dead and paralysed another. They fled to Houston and were involved in a gunfight with police, before being arrested. Thomas stood trial in Dallas and was sentenced to death.

The first time I met Thomas, he was being interviewed by a pretty little blonde journalist from Denmark. I introduced myself and we hit it off immediately. Because he'd always come down and talk to any reporter who wanted to talk to him, he made my life easier as a result. He always told the same stories, but he gave a pretty good interview. I'd sit on his bunk with him, chat with him in the garment factory. He was an avid basketball fan, and I'd shoot hoops with him in the recreation area, before Martin Gurule ruined it for everybody and death row was locked down. I always joked that he should wear handcuffs, to make the game more even. I liked Thomas a lot. I soon got past the fact he was an offender, he was just a person.

Back in the 1980s, Dallas wasn't a good place for black people to be accused of murder, because of an explicit instruction from District Attorney Henry Wade to keep minorities off jury panels. My old attorney friend, who it transpired was a special prosecutor and not a regular defence attorney, contended that Thomas had an unfair murder trial, because the jury had been stacked against him through the deliberate exclusion of black people. I explained to these attorneys that Thomas was pretty much a peacemaker in prison and had resolved some touchy situations between other offenders. There's an old adage that the best prisoners are murderers, because with most of them it was a one-off crime, and it wasn't planned, it just happened. Often, they turned out to be no problem at all, and that's what Thomas was like. He was pretty much a member of 'The Broke Dick Club', which is a prison term for old inmates who can't work much and get assigned jobs like crushing cans for recycling. Time in a penitentiary is going to change you, and some of these guys became better people. Thomas was one of them, he was no longer a threat to society.

These attorneys took my stories back to the judge, and Thomas' sentence was commuted to life in prison. Thomas turned down the opportunity of a second murder trial, because the guy he paralysed was still around and would have testified against him.

I never asked Thomas if he was guilty or not. I knew what he was supposed to have done, and he knew I knew. But I was never convinced he was the trigger man, I always suspected he took the rap for his wife Dorothy. But it didn't matter to me whether Thomas had done the crime or not. What mattered to me was that Thomas was not given due process in court. Getting him off death row made me feel good, I felt wonderful about it. But after a while, I started thinking, 'Did I do the right thing? Have I done Thomas any favours? Probably not.' Thomas will never get out of prison alive, he'll be taken out feet first.

In my eight years at TDCJ, I became very aware of the suffering offenders went through, not just on death row but in the general population. It's not a good life in prison. In fact, it's a horrible existence in one of those hell holes. In Texas prisons, the rate of attempted suicide is incredibly high, but the amount of successful suicides is low. That tells me two things: first, prison in Texas is a very bad place to be; second, the prison system is ruthlessly efficient.

Word soon got out that I was a good expert witness, and I suddenly started getting emails and phone calls from defence lawyers all over Texas. I never considered myself to be an expert in anything, and all of a sudden I discovered I was. I guess I left TDCJ with a PhD in prison life. I'd stand in court and explain how the system worked, what an offender's existence would be like if he got life instead of death. It was essentially my job to explain to that panel of 12 people that there was an alternative to killing the offender. What's really funny is that I started working alongside a guy named Dennis Longmire, who was a criminal justice professor at Sam Houston State and staunchly anti-death penalty. Dennis protested outside the Walls Unit on the day of every execution, come rain or come shine. I respected him a lot, and now we were on the same team.

In a couple of trials I testified at, the jury voted for capital life rather than capital death. But I didn't do it out of any ethical considerations, I did it because it kept me busy and was good money. And I never really thought that I was testifying against the death penalty, to the extent that I always wondered why I never got approached by any prosecutors, because the information I provided could have just as well been applied by them.

I experienced love from offenders' families and a lot of hate and hostility from victims' families, as well as some of my old colleagues in the prison system. I went back to Huntsville for a retirement party, and one of the wardens called me a traitor. I thought, 'Piss on him if he thinks I'm a traitor, I don't give a shit what he or anybody else thinks, because I've always been loyal to the prison system, despite all its flaws.' I was proud of my duty with TDCJ, I did not do them a disservice.

At a murder trial in Livingston, I was asked how I felt about the death penalty, and I gave my stock reply: 'It's not germane how I feel about the death penalty.' This attorney jumped up and said, 'Mr Fitzgerald, it is germane when I ask you under oath!' So I said, 'Yeah, I favour it, but we use it too much in Texas.' The offender had killed his girlfriend, who was considerably older than he was, and seemed truly remorseful. But it was a slam-dunk for the prosecution, and he ended up getting the death sentence.

As time went on, I started to question the point of the death penalty more and more. Certainly, revenge had a lot to do with it. In Texas, a lot of prosecutors have a notch-on-the-belt, cowboy mentality. Being a district attorney in Texas is a political job, and they like to be seen as tough on crime and protecting the community. Henry Wade, who was Dallas County District Attorney for 36 years, had a 93 per cent conviction rate, and defence attorneys who managed a rare win against him called themselves 'The 7% Club'. That's the mentality.

There is also the question of cost. It's very expensive to execute somebody, and most people don't understand that. If you get the death penalty in Texas, the appeal is automatic, so you then have to go through the federal appellate court, and with an assortment of other appeals you can file all the way up to the US Supreme Court. By the time that person is strapped to the gurney, millions of dollars will have been spent. When Lawrence Brewer and John King were sentenced to death in the Jasper dragging case, Jasper County had to hike property taxes to pay for it.

But what worried me more than cost was the spate of exonerations. In the seven years after Wade died in 2001, there were 19 in Dallas County alone, two-thirds involving black people, usually as a result of DNA testing. Michael Morton was in a Texas prison for almost 25 years after being convicted of beating his wife to death. His attorneys fought for six years to get them to test for DNA, and when the results came back, Morton was found to be innocent. Not only that, there was some suggestion that the Williamson County District Attorney had withheld evidence that allowed the actual murderer to go free and kill again. Ernest Willis spent 17 years on death row after being found guilty of setting a fire that killed two women. He came close to being executed in 1991, before being cleared of all charges and released in 2004. They're still arguing over whether Cameron Todd Willingham set the fire that killed his three daughters, and he was executed the same year Willis walked free.

A number of people have been let off death row, which tells me the system has flaws. Testifying in capital murder trials, I saw some real questionable things done by prosecutors. They'd bring in expert witnesses who'd testify that a guy given a life sentence would likely kill again, so he should be executed instead. One of them made it sound like there was blood flowing down the aisles of the prison units. I found it somewhat troubling that one of the criteria for getting the death penalty was 'future dangerousness'. These are people who would have no contact with people on death row, eat their food in their cell, have one hour of recreation a day. How could they possibly be a future danger to anybody? And having worked for an agency that committed the ultimate bureaucratic act, it made me think, 'Did they always get it right?' I didn't feel guilty, I didn't do anything to put those people on death row, but I hated to think I'd seen people executed who were innocent.

I kept up friendships with former inmates, which is not something I thought would happen. We'd write back and forth and occasionally I'd get a phone call out of the blue. They were like the conversations you'd have with someone you went to school with – 'hey, what's going on?' – and I thought it was great that these people were managing to live lives outside of prison. There was one young inmate I knew who had a car wreck on the day he graduated high school and killed some teenagers. Before that night, he'd never had a drink in his life. There but for the grace of God go I. During his time in prison, I got to like him a lot. He was just a frail human being like me who made a mistake, but at least it wasn't a mistake he had to die for. When he got out, me and Marianne even went on a tubing trip with him and his family. He earned a college degree in prison and wound up working as an attorney. After I retired, I once tried to visit Thomas Miller-El, but they said I wasn't allowed in. I'm not sure why, I only wanted to see an old friend.

In 2015, I got a call from the BBC in England. They wanted to make a documentary about me watching all those executions. One day, the director asked me, 'Would you consider talking to Napoleon

Beazley's parents on camera?' I said, 'Sure, but they won't do it.' He called me back the next day and told me they wanted to. On the way out to their house in Grapeland, it suddenly occurred to me that I had no real idea about Napoleon's background. I knew he was bright and a star footballer, but I didn't know if he lived in a shack or something more salubrious. It turned out they lived in a beautiful big house in the country, which surprised me somewhat.

I was apprehensive, because I thought they'd be angry or upset. But it turned out they were a real nice couple. It was a heck of an afternoon. Napoleon's father Ireland seemed real bitter at the system, but after the interview was over, he told me he was a correctional officer. The irony of that floored me. His wife Rena was a real sweet person. She described Napoleon as 'a son that everyone would want to have', who used to treat her like a queen and introduce her as 'his woman'. The whole time he was on death row, they never missed a visit. When I told her how attached I was to Napoleon, she started crying and really opened up. I was surprised when she told me she was not opposed to the death penalty, for the worst of the worst. Then again, that wasn't what Napoleon was. She told me the fact I was there for Napoleon's execution gave her comfort, which was nice to hear. That's how I wanted to be remembered, as a guy who treated everybody fairly.

When TDCJ put the big squeeze on Michelle, it made me angry. She didn't deserve what happened to her. Michelle and I were very close, I liked her an awful lot. She treated the inmates like human beings and the reporters as equals, just like I did. That's why they stabbed her in the back and got rid of her, because they saw her as belonging to the old way of doing things. She was open and helpful and curious, while the TDCJ wanted to close things down. After Michelle left, they stopped telling the public about riots and escapes and hostage situations. Did all those nasty things suddenly stop happening? Or did they just start hiding things? As one of my old TDCJ colleagues said to me, 'It's like they turned off the faucet.' I guess Michelle gave the prison system in Texas more honesty and publicity than it wanted.

When we were both there, we'd walk up this little flight of stairs that led from the parking lot and I'd sweep my arm across the Walls Unit and say, 'Miss Lyons, one day this will all be yours...' But I felt guilty about hiring her, not only because of how it ended, but because of the effect watching all those executions had had on me. After I left, I couldn't stop thinking about the things I'd seen. And when a beautiful carol like 'Silent Night' makes you think about death, something's definitely not right. I'd have dreams about Karla Faye Tucker and Gary Graham and Kenneth McDuff. Kenneth McDuff is not somebody you want to be dreaming about, but that man was etched on my mind for all time.

I'd dream about things that were said in last statements, like the guy who recited that long passage from Corinthians. I'd dream about eating bing cherries in the death house with James Beathard. I'd dream about a kid they named 'Sweat Pea', a harmless-looking guy who killed a cop. He'd been involved in a shoot-out and had complications from his wounds, so they sent him to hospital in Galveston, gave him *an operation, brought him back and executed him. I'd have these dreams several times a week, but I didn't talk about it a whole lot. I might tell my wife a funny convict story, but not the bad stuff. I kept that locked up.*

I didn't have hobbies, didn't play golf. I joined a gym once but never went. Work was what I did and what I liked. I enjoyed retirement for a while, because every day was like Saturday. But as I got older, I had more and more spare time on my hands, and spare time means thinking. And thinking all those thoughts made an addiction worse. I started drinking more and more, medicating myself earlier and earlier in the day, before heading to a bar. That was partly out of boredom, partly to forget.

There was a time when I read scripture, I was even an altar boy as a kid. I drifted away from organised religion, but kept my beliefs. When I became ill, Jim Brazzil would call and we'd have long talks about God and what might happen when I died. I often asked him, 'Could you feel the inmate's soul leaving their body, when you had your hand on their knee?' Brazzil said that it was a deeply intense moment, and assured me that he could feel the inmate entering the presence of God. I saw 219 inmates die on that gurney, but it wasn't the executions I remembered that bothered me the most, it was the executions I'd forgotten...

I was upset when I discovered Larry felt guilty about hiring me, because I didn't blame him at all. He was the most wonderful man, and the best spokesperson the prison system ever had. We were both members of this weird little club, which nobody asks to join.

There aren't too many people on the planet who know what it's like to see that many executions. The wardens came and went, members of the tie-down team came and went, members of the IV team came and went. Everybody came and went, except for me, Larry, Chaplain Brazzil and Graczyk. But even Graczyk wasn't an active member of the club, because he was still witnessing executions, and was never going to discuss his feelings about them until he retired.

When my executive director had asked how I walked into that death chamber to watch a man die, I thought, 'You think you couldn't handle watching an execution? Then why aren't you concerned about sending me in there almost 300 times?' But I can't really be mad at him for that. I didn't want to share my duties with anyone, because I didn't think that anyone could do it better than me. I don't know if that sounds arrogant or not, but it never even crossed my mind. And even if they'd offered me professional help, I would have declined, because accepting help would have been a show of weakness. And if you admit any kind of weakness in that job, they're going to pull you out of the firing line.

Nevertheless, one day it occurred to me that I'd seen an awful lot of executions and had nobody to talk to. How could any therapist help me, when they'd never seen any executions themselves? So I started recording voice memos during my commutes. I'd fish my phone from my bag, press the red button and just start talking. I didn't know what I was going to do with the recordings, or even why I was making them. But I guess it was a way of cataloguing my thoughts, just as I'd done with my execution journal. When I'm lying in bed at night, thinking of all the things I need to do, I have to switch on the light and write them down, otherwise I'll worry they'll just lurk instead, in the nooks of my mind. It was a similar process with the recordings. I'd accepted that I'd never forget some of the executions I'd witnessed, but at least if I knew they were filed away neatly, they wouldn't be able to creep up and spook me.

> 'I thought being away from the prison system would make me think about it less, but it's been quite the opposite. I think about it all the time. Now that I'm gone, it's like I've taken the lid off Pandora's Box and I can't put it back on.'
>
> **Michelle's voice memo, November 2012**

CHAPTER 13
NO MONOPOLY ON GRIEF

'If you come to Texas and kill somebody, we will kill you back.'

Ron White, Texan comedian and actor

'I don't wear no Stetson,

But I'm willin' to bet, son,

That I'm as big a Texan as you are.'

Terry Allen, *Amarillo Highway*

I always just wanted a normal life – a good husband, kids, a dog, a nice house, a job that pays me enough money that I can travel further afield than Texas. Some of that I have now, some of it I don't. I read a quote once: 'People always ask me, "Why do you always take the hard road?" And I replied, "Why do you assume I see more than one road?"' That resonated with me, because that's always the way it seems to be in my life. It's not that I want to do things the hard way, it just ends up being like that.

I ignored red flags before my second marriage, and ploughed on regardless. Once again, I only saw the hard road. As with my job in the prison system, I don't expect or want anybody to feel sorry for me, because I knew what it was going into it.

I have a beautiful daughter, great parents, a wonderful brother who I'm very close to, great families on both sides, but I wasted too much time on certain relationships. My child knows how to read me like a book and I have some great friends who know just about everything there is to know about me. But in my romantic life, I've tended to fall short, ending up with men who didn't understand me and my quirks and the various traits that make me who I am.

I don't really get it, other than maybe they weren't really paying attention, because I give all sorts of clues that a good detective would spot, if only they were looking.

Take my tattoos. I got my first when I was 18, stone-cold sober and all by myself, a fleur-de-lis on my big toe. The fleur-de-lis was the symbol of my college sorority, but what's funny is, I wasn't a very active member. I didn't live in the house like many of my pledge sisters, and I missed a lot of meetings because of my job at the local newspaper, yet I was probably one of the only members who got themselves inked. Other tattoos include an evil eye, a nod to my Hispanic and Greek heritage and to ward off bad energy, jealousy and negativity; the Chinese symbol for strength; and a flaming heart that speaks to the fact that I love wildly and deeply. I also have a butterfly, which I got for a little poem I read, which was actually a Japanese Geisha song:

I know she is light and faithless,
But she has come back half-repentant
And very pale and very sad.
A butterfly needs somewhere to rest
At evening.

On my side, in gothic cursive, is the phrase, '*Alea iacta est*', or 'The die is cast'. I got that one during a particularly stressful time in my life, when I was spending a lot of time worrying about how

NO MONOPOLY ON GRIEF \ 265

things would turn out. That tattoo was a way of reminding myself that worrying was useless, because fate had already decided the outcome. On my other side, I have an anchor, with a banner across it that reads 'Mother'. I got that one shortly after my beloved grandmother died, and it's a tribute to all the strong mothers in my life: my own mother, my grandmothers, my aunts and cousins, and the next generation – my daughter, niece and my cousins' girls. The anchor also speaks to my Galveston Island roots – a nautical symbol for my nautical home.

I have not one, but two black widow tattoos. In 2002, I started the tongue-in-cheek 'Black Widow Club', which is made up of a bunch of strong women I know and love – not man-haters or women who plot to kill their mates, like Betty Lou Beets, but women who are tough and fierce. The club has eight members, and we all have the tattoo. I like being president of my own club, even if it's one I had to invent myself.

Since most of my tattoos aren't visible in public, a person trying to figure out who I am should simply look at the tangled clutter of bracelets that adorn my wrists: an anchor, that matches one I gave my father, who is the giver of so much advice; one that reads, 'Rebellious When Restricted'; a string bracelet with a little gold snake, that is actually a wish bracelet – you put it on, make a wish and when the string wears away and falls off, your wish is ready to come true; a bracelet with a heart, which matches one worn by my mother, who does everything she possibly can to lift me when I'm down; a silver bear claw, matching one worn by my brother, who is one of my best friends and fiercely loyal; a silver cross, which is a gift from my daughter; an assortment of evil eye bracelets; and a silver bracelet, on which is stamped, 'I will try again tomorrow'.

The clues aren't exactly buried in the undergrowth, but maybe that's part of the problem. Sometimes I worry I'm too much: too honest, too deep, too expressive, too loving, too worried about appearing strong. But I don't know how to be anything else: if I don't say the things I feel when I feel them, then I am not being me. Will the real me have a happily ever after? Or is that just not in my cards? But apart from the odd twinge of regret, I wouldn't change a thing (except perhaps that *Today Show* interview, in which I sounded like an insensitive hick), because every decision I've made has brought me to this point in my life, in which I'm happy and content.

Had I not worked for the prison system for all those years, I might have had more peace, but I wouldn't have the amazing job I have now, working with great people, taking trips to London, rather than a baking hot prison in the wilds of Texas, meeting rapists and baby killers. And I might not have my daughter, the most important thing that will ever happen to me.

If there is nothing else I ever get right, I am so proud of my daughter. I needn't have worried that the darkness would rub off on her when she was growing inside my belly and I was listening to the last words of the inmates – their anger, their despair, their fear.

She is so light and funny and kind-hearted. I think that's what you most hope for as a parent, that your child will be better than you in every way. We were on a cruise and I watched as she began talking to this kid who looked miserable and alone. She brought him into her group and soon they were running around like the oldest of friends. I am so proud that she is without limits or judgement, and embraces and celebrates everyone for who they are.

But my daughter also brings into sharper focus how the women who walked into the death chamber must have felt – both those watching their sons die, and those watching their children's killers go to sleep. I have an eager anticipation to see how her story unfolds, whereas the inmates' mothers watch as the story comes to an end. Every single hope and desire they had for their baby is snuffed out, right in front of them. And I'm sure they question where they went wrong, as irrational as that might be.

Come to my house and you'll see lots of crosses, skulls and *santos* dolls dotted about, which some people might find macabre. When I was working for the Israeli Consulate, a colleague brought his son in and said, 'This is the woman who used to work for the prison system', and made me show him all this memorabilia that was on my desk, including a shank I used as an envelope opener, and these tiny dice made out of compacted toilet paper. And I still find crime as fascinating as I did when I first joined the prison system. My ideal Sunday evening's viewing is a combination of *Dateline* and *48 Hours*, with maybe a show about ghosts and the paranormal, after my daughter has gone to bed. But I don't come across as a weird or dark person, even though I might think some weird, dark things.

Sometimes, when I'm in a crowded bar, I'll look around and think, 'You know, statistically, someone in here has committed a murder.' Or I'll look at someone and think, 'Hmmm, he looks like a sex offender.' There will just be something about someone that makes me suspicious. Working in the prison system also made me more cautious of people. I'd sit in on reporters' interviews with burglars and muggers and pick up all kinds of tips. One guy, who was really funny to listen to, said that if he was walking past your house and the garage door was open, he was leaving with something, whether it was a set of golf clubs, a lawnmower, your tool box or a bag of charcoal.

I'm not afraid to go anywhere, but I'm constantly looking behind me and locking doors. When I arrive at a parking lot, you won't see me digging around in my bag for my car keys, they will already be in my hand. I was relieved to discover that my new car had an escape lever in the trunk. I thank my lucky stars that I have small hands and wrists, so that if I'm ever snapped in handcuffs, I'll probably be able to squeeze out of them. I don't want to make my daughter paranoid or afraid to leave the house, but I probably think about kidnapping and sex trafficking more than the average mom, and I want her to be cautious. But it's a fine line. I'll be watching a crime documentary and she'll be looking up serial killers on the internet – 'Mama, look at this one! He killed 20 people!' Is that right? Probably not. But

I want her to realise that just because somebody looks nice, that doesn't necessarily mean they are nice. There are so many people who do so many bad things in the world, and because of the job I did, I know exactly the kinds of bad things they do.

On 6 January 2016, my husband and I were watching television when he said something that made me laugh so hard I could barely breathe. About two minutes later, my cell phone rang. It was my husband's oldest daughter, Lacey, but because we were in the middle of watching a show and having so much fun, I decided to ignore it and call her back. About a minute later, I got a text which read: 'Please. Kristine is dead.' Kristine was my husband's youngest daughter. My stomach knotted up. I thought perhaps that Lacey was being dramatic, that she couldn't get hold of her sister and was assuming the worst. I asked my husband where his phone was, and he said it was in our bedroom on the charger. When he asked me why, I read him the text, he ran to the bedroom, grabbed his phone, called Lacey and then all I could hear was her screaming. That's when I knew it was true.

Soon, the story of a 17-year-old girl from Houston being shot dead in a Los Angeles parking lot was all over Twitter. People were posting pictures of this girl who had been in my house six months earlier, celebrating her birthday. From covering all those murders as a reporter, to seeing 280 people executed, now I was part of the story, watching it from almost the opening page. I wasn't particularly close to Kristine, had not been around her a ton, because she had only come back into my husband's life a year or so earlier. But it's not like it didn't affect me. My worst fear as a parent was being played out in front of me. And watching my husband go through all that pain and suffering was harrowing and heartbreaking in equal measure.

Kristine was shot in the face by a drug dealer in Marina del Rey, after a botched drug deal involving Lacey's boyfriend. I knew the death penalty wouldn't be on the table, because California hasn't executed anybody since 2006. But my husband struggled to grasp that, and it was stressful trying to get him to come to terms with the fact that it was never going to happen. Death was all he and Kristine's mother wanted, the only palatable outcome.

In July 2017, Kristine's killer was sentenced to life without parole. I knew it was coming and yet I felt angry at the injustice. God only knows how my husband felt. For years I'd been arguing about the death penalty at parties, with people for whom it was an abstract concept. But if I thought it was a concrete issue for me while I was working for the prison system, my stepdaughter's murder only hardened my position. While there were executions I saw that I didn't agree with and executions I saw that I wish I had not, I maintain that there are instances when the death penalty is an appropriate punishment for the taking of a human life. And if anyone has the balls to stand there and tell me why the death penalty is wrong, they should be prepared to hear my very personal take on why I think they are mistaken.

If their 17-year-old daughter was shot in the face and killed, how would they cope knowing that her killer's life was spared? I know, from personal experience, that it is a bitter pill to swallow.

When I think it's all dealt with, I'll suddenly find myself crying at something seemingly innocuous. I went to see *Murder on the Orient Express*, which is one of my favourite Agatha Christie tales, and started sobbing in the theatre. Who the hell cries during an Agatha Christie movie? What I took away from this new adaptation is that sometimes one murder can cause everything around it to unravel – even if only one person is physically buried, they might not be the only person who died. That's exactly what happened when my stepdaughter was murdered, because my husband never recovered. I loved him dearly, but he became a different man. Not long after Kristine's death, I discovered he had developed a serious drug habit, which I would not tolerate in my home. We divorced in no time at all, and I haven't seen him since.

When I got back from seeing *Murder on the Orient Express*, I opened up my laptop and started drafting a letter to the man who shot my now ex-husband's daughter. I wanted him to know that he didn't just kill her, he killed my husband's spirit. And over what? Some fucking weed. I didn't end up writing the letter, let alone sending it, because I'm not sure he would have cared.

Around the same time, I received a message on Facebook, from a friend of a man I saw executed. I didn't remember much about him, so I had to pull his notes from the filing cabinet in my office to jog my memory. He was sentenced to death for a carjacking and murder in Houston in 1992. The offender was 19 at the time. In the news articles, the victim's daughter was quoted as saying she really lost both her parents that day, because her mother went into a deep depression that she never really came out of. But here was this message on my phone, reminding me that the offender's execution altered the lives of his family and friends, too. These were people who didn't commit a crime, but were still scrutinised and judged as if they did. And then their loved one was executed.

Her message read:

'I am writing to you in hope that you can help me put my heart and mind at ease. I believe that you witnessed the execution of someone who was like my family. I knew him since I was 12 years old. I just want to know that he went quickly and that he did not suffer. I love him now as I loved him then. I hope that you answer. His name was Willie Marcel Shannon #999086. He was executed Nov 8 2006. If you don't answer I will understand. Thank you and God bless you.'

I wrote back to Shannon's old friend and told her he died quickly and without pain. In fact, I told her what I'd told so many people down the years, that it looked like he went to sleep. I also told her that he was smiling on the gurney, said he would ask for the victim's forgiveness when he saw him in heaven and that he would be waiting for his mother when she got there. Shannon wasn't afraid of dying, and his faith was very much intact. I don't know if my reply was too stoic, or whether it brought her peace or comfort, but it seemed like the right thing to do. There is no monopoly on grief.

If I had been veering towards an anti-death penalty position, the murder of my stepdaughter sent me swerving the other way again. But there are signs that Texas is losing its appetite for the ultimate punishment. Harris County, which includes Houston, America's fourth most populous city, was known as the 'capital of capital punishment', having sent 126 convicts to death row since the death penalty was reinstated in 1976. However, in 2017, Harris County executed none of its death row inmates for the first time since 1985, and did not sentence anybody to death for the third year in a row. Seven executions took place in Huntsville in 2017, the same as the previous year and down from the record 40 in 2000.

Among the reasons for the dip are the 2005 introduction of life without parole; reformist district attorneys and prosecutors; better defence lawyers; jurors who are more understanding of mitigating circumstances for an alleged killer's crime, such as an abusive childhood or mental illness; the school of thought that it can't possibly be a deterrent, given that there is still so much violent crime; a host of recent DNA exonerations; botched executions in other states; the difficulty in acquiring the necessary drugs; the huge cost of pursuing a death penalty; and a growing belief that execution should be spared for the worst of the worst.

But while a 2017 Gallup poll suggested that public support for the death penalty for murder across America was down to 55 per cent, the lowest in 45 years and way down from the 1994 peak of 80 per cent, the last major poll in Texas, in 2013, suggested that public support remained strong, at 74 per cent. So long as Texas has so many crazy people committing so many crazy crimes, no Texas politician will be campaigning on an anti-death penalty platform, at least not one who wants to be elected. Crime and punishment is big business in the state, Texas has its own way of doing things, and it doesn't really care what anybody else thinks. It's like that saying: 'Texas is like a whole other country'.

'I support the death penalty. I believe there are some crimes that are so heinous, the only way you can truly pay your debt to society is with your life. But in other cases, I feel very conflicted. There are men I watched die that I don't think should have. But I have that luxury, because they didn't take something from me.'

Michelle voice memo, November 2012

Maybe I participated in too many things I shouldn't have. Maybe you can't be so close to so much badness and negativity without it tainting everything you do in the future. Maybe I'll never escape the things I saw. I used to think that when I died, I'd want them to play the Green Day song 'Good Riddance', because I like the words and the message, and thought it would look funny printed in the funeral programme. But on one commute home, Eva Cassidy's 'Songbird' came on the radio, and I realised that was the song I wanted at my funeral instead. But you know what made me sad? There's a line that says, 'And the songbirds keep singing like they know the score', which I must have heard a hundred times. But this was the first time I realised it meant score, as in melody. I'd always interpreted it as the score in the game of the life – your score against the universe. Why would I think that? Why is that what I hear? Why am I so afraid that the universe is keeping score and that, no matter what, I'm going to lose? As I listened, I cried, because I want people to know that I really did try to do right and not cause any hurt. And, for the first time, I got the feeling that I wasn't going to live to be an old woman, that I was going to die young, with so many things undone and so much unredeemed. Suddenly I knew the score, and it wasn't a melody at all.

When I was younger, I thought that witnessing people die would have no lasting effect on me. I didn't consider that life is fluid, you're constantly growing, and just because you feel a certain way about something one day, it doesn't mean you'll feel that way for ever. That *Rolling Stone* journalist was wrong, but kind of right at the same time: it's not that I saw too much death for somebody of my age, but I did end up seeing too much death for anyone. I can't figure out if I was strong for doing it for so long or I'm weak for the feelings I still harbour. Maybe it's both.

Sometimes I wonder if instead of trying to file things away, it might be a better course of action to shout it from the rooftops. Before I started writing this book, I didn't really know why I was doing it. But perhaps that's it: I'm trying to desensitise myself to the things I've seen. My husband and I had a song, and I loved that song so much that when we separated, I didn't want to retire it, shut it away in a box, close the lid and never listen to it again. So I kept listening to it after he was gone, over and over again, so I could desensitise myself to it. Eventually, I'd listened to it so often that it didn't mean anything any more. It just went back to being a song I really liked. Maybe this book will achieve something similar.

CHAPTER 14
A DAY WITHOUT SUNSHINE

'But I am old; and good and bad
Are woven in a crazy plaid.
I sit and say, "The world is so;
And he is wise who lets it go".'

Dorothy Parker, excerpt from *The Veteran*

One of the things that made Larry such a tremendous public information officer was his ability to shine during a stressful situation, keep calm when everything around him was chaos and keep panic at bay. So it wasn't a huge surprise that when he fell ill in the fall of 2016, he downplayed it. He simply told me he wasn't feeling well, had decided to give up drinking, and was having some blood tests run. Nothing alarming, apart from the bit about giving up drinking.

It was left to his wife Marianne to tell me the real story. The years of alcohol use had caught up with Larry and his liver was failing, which would eventually cause him to die. Nothing short of a liver transplant could stop that from happening, and he thought liver transplants should be saved for younger, more deserving people. Larry's father had died when he was a child, so I don't think he expected to last that long anyway. Luckily, he had his mother's constitution and just felt privileged to have lived a wonderful life.

There are some characters who loom so large in your life that it never occurs to you what you might do if something bad befalls them. That's how I felt about Larry. I wasn't sure how to process the idea of losing him, because he had always seemed so strong.

I couldn't imagine a world without him in it, and I did my best not to try. I carried on just as I always had, calling him every now and again, sending him funny text messages. For years he'd joked that his liver probably resembled a smoked oyster, and now I was quick to remind him that he'd been right all along. When Marianne told me he was asking for all sorts of funky food in hospital, I sent him a message reminding him that he wasn't on death row and therefore not required to request 12 fried eggs, three pork chops, a pint of ice cream and a cheeseburger. In one message he told me he 'should have smoked dope and left the booze alone', which sounded like a pretty good title for a country music album.

He seemed mildly irritated that he'd had to sell his Japanese hot rod, but genuinely excited about this book and anxious that we didn't leave any good stories out. He even suggested a title: 'A day without an execution is like a day without sunshine.' He was, of course, being ironic. He even had the energy to aim a few jabs at TDCJ, telling me he hoped he lived to see the day that Jason Clark loses his job and 'is forced to go into precious metals... picking up cans along Interstate 45'.

All the while, Larry was getting weaker and weaker, not that I knew it. Occasionally, he'd mention in passing that he wasn't feeling well, but again, it was up to Marianne to fill in the blanks. In March 2017, I visited Larry at his home in Austin. He had lost so much weight that his withered body was drowning in an oversized flannel shirt. He was confined to a wheelchair, too weak to walk around freely on his own. His voice, once loud and clear, was mostly a whisper. We spoke for a few hours about executions, me recording his thoughts and recollections. And the entire time, the clock kept moving forward to the moment I most dreaded, when I would have to say goodbye, knowing it would most likely be for the last time.

I made it through the day without crying, until I stood up to leave. When I bent down to give him a hug, I couldn't keep my tears at bay any longer. As I sobbed against his shoulder, he told me simply, 'You've always been a good kid.' And with that, I left. There were more texts, but the time between each one grew longer and longer. Finally, he stopped answering at all. He lived on for a couple more months, but spent most of that time sleeping, until he finally died in June.

Larry's memorial was held on a hot Friday afternoon in the community centre of his suburban Austin neighbourhood. Me and a few friends of Marianne arranged a reception and dozens of people came, bearing all types of savoury dishes and desserts and, of course, wine and beer. It was a casual affair, just as Larry would have wanted. Marianne and their two kids, Kelly and Kevin, mingled with old friends and colleagues, and a couple of reporters who had managed to sneak away from deadlines dropped by to pay their respects. Then it was time for some stories.

An old room-mate from Larry's bachelor days told us that Larry got them kicked out of four or five apartments for doing all sorts of crazy crap. One time, Larry was running a bath when a couple of cute girls from down the corridor invited him out for drinks. He returned to find their soaked belongings strewn over the front lawn, along with an eviction notice. Then it was my turn. I told them about the time Larry marched me past the naked inmates; the time he made me eat food loaf; the fact he called me 'Little Larry' and made fun of me for my woefully inadequate vocabulary. And just as I was starting to settle in, my voice started to shake, as it had when I left Larry that final time. Just as then, I didn't know how to say goodbye. But I did manage to say, 'There will never be another like him', which is the absolute truth.

When the memorial was over, an old colleague from our prison days produced a small bottle of Scotch – one of Larry's preferred brands – and poured us all a shot. We toasted our dear friend and then it was time to go home. It was my dad who summed it up best, likening Fitzgerald's death to a famous line in the classic American movie *The Big Lebowski*, which he and Larry both adored: 'It's good knowin' he's out there'. That's how we all felt about Larry. It was just good knowing he was out there, and it hurts knowing he's not.

Larry Fitzgerald's obituary, by Larry Fitzgerald

'Born in Austin, Texas on October 12, 1937, Larry Fitzgerald touched the third rail on June 12, 2017.

Larry was a graduate of Austin's McCallum High School and the University of Texas. He worked for numerous Texas radio stations as a newsman, gatherer and news director, before becoming director of communications for the State Bar of Texas. He worked in political campaigns for Lt. Governor Bill Hobby and Governor Ann Richards.

Larry perhaps was best known for his role as public information officer for the Texas Department of Criminal Justice (the free world's largest gulag) in Huntsville, Texas. In that capacity, Larry witnessed 219 executions, allowing him to meet many state, national and international media types. Big whoop. He won some awards – some merited, some not. He was a regular blood donor, often said to have a very rare blood type – the only one that could be used to jump-start a wino. He volunteered at Meals on Wheels and the Bullock Museum and was recognized as Volunteer of the Year at KUT Radio.

Upon his official retirement from TDCJ, Larry was hired as an expert witness to testify on behalf of the defense during the punishment phase of more than 30 capital murder cases. He was successful in some cases and in others, not so.

Larry's departure from TDCJ was not the end of his state service. Larry worked for the Texas Division of Emergency Management, advising on the response to floods, fires and hurricanes, and he also enjoyed working for the Texas Secretary of the Senate during each legislative session from 2005 to 2013. He was hired to conduct location shooting for the now-defunct Texas Department of Commerce in an ambitious effort to lure major movie-makers to shoot their productions in Texas. It was an interesting job that allowed him the opportunity to see miles and miles of Texas, a state he dearly loved.

Larry is survived by his long-suffering wife Marianne Cook

Fitzgerald, who he always lovingly referred to as his "Child Bride", as well as his daughter, Kelly Anne Fitzgerald, his son Kevin Lane Fitzgerald and his spouse Lorraine Fitzgerald, all of Austin. He also is survived by his shepherd/heeler rescue dog, Charlie, who was a comfort provider and travel companion.

Larry was preceded in death by his father, Clyde Jackson Fitzgerald of San Marcos, and his beloved mother, Dorothy Tillman Fitzgerald of Smithville, Texas.

Larry worked diligently to support the economies of Kentucky, Ireland, Great Britain, Scotland and Mexico. He never met a bartender he didn't like, which is why his liver looked like a smoked oyster. He was proud that he kept one particular promise he had made to himself: never vote Republican.

EPILOGUE
MY JOB TO REMEMBER?

After my second divorce, I went to change my driver's licence back to my maiden name. I was filling out all the paperwork in my neat and purposeful handwriting and came to where it asked for my two emergency contacts. I put my mom and dad. I was a 41-year-old single mom with two failed marriages under her belt, whose parents would be called if I died in a car crash, because I had nobody else to make arrangements or grieve for me. When my number was called, I joked with the woman behind the counter about how glad I was to be divorced, so I could get a new photo on my licence. Then I sat in my car and cried, because I felt more alone than I had in a very long time.

That fear of being forgotten was still deep within me. For so many years, that 16-year-old boy from high school, who left me devastated by moving on so soon, had convinced me I was easily discarded. But when I really thought about some of the most significant relationships I'd had, I realised that was never true. I was never immediately forgotten, there was never a clean break, people always tried to come back, and I never left anyone who didn't ask for another chance. They all wanted to hang on to at least a part of me. One old boyfriend recently said that he sometimes pictures me driving along with the windows down, singing along to a particular song on the radio. I didn't remember that at all, but I loved that that was how I existed in his mind. And I finally realised that I had confused a hormonal boy who just wanted to spend the summer with a girl, any girl, with being easy to forget or insignificant. I let the misconceptions of that naïve, impressionable teenage girl colour my world for decades and bleed into other parts of my life. Why should I care if someone remembers me or not? I started telling myself, 'You know what? You have your shit together, you really do bring a lot of stuff to the table. If they tear you up and forget about you, that's their problem.

'Time to take stock and move on.'

*

Peckerwood Hill, where Texas prisoners have been buried for more than 150 years, is a peaceful place on a fine summer's day, somewhat creepy when the weather isn't so great. It is also a memorial to wasted lives and what it truly means to be forgotten. You don't see many flowers on graves at Peckerwood Hill. If you die in prison in Huntsville and nobody wants your remains, chances are this is where you'll wind up. Hundreds of dead men and women lie beneath unmarked crosses, a relic from the days when nobody cared if you had ever lived, let alone died on their watch. Nowadays, if you were an inmate in the general population, they'll furnish you with a solid headstone made by other inmates, and with your name and date of death painted on in crude lettering. Until recently, if you were executed, all you were afforded was a date of death, your prison number and an 'X', a symbol that you'll never escape the horror of your crime. If you were executed today, they'd at least include your name.

But none of the headstones contain clues as to when they came into the world, where they died or why they wound up in prison in the first place. If you were a con artist or a car thief, you might end up buried next to a rapist or a baby killer. On a recent visit, I noticed the headstone of a Tillman Simmons, which tells me he was led to the electric chair on 26 September 1927. Google tells me he was sentenced to death for the murder of a man named Frank Usry, in Bexar County on 20 August 1924. Except that it wasn't Simmons who shot Usry, but his accomplice Matthew Briscoe. Would I have given Simmons the death penalty? Probably not.

Not far from Simmons' grave is that of George Hassell, who killed his wife and eight children on the night of 5 December 1926, with a hammer, a razor, some stockings, an axe and a shotgun. He was sent to 'Old Sparky' on 10 February 1928, and I'd say he's rotting in hell. About 50 yards away from Simmons lies Thomas Mason, the man who reminded me of my grandpa. When Mason was arrested, he laughed and said, 'I don't know what the big deal is over just getting rid of my mother-in-law.' I think he probably deserved what he got. A few rows from Mason is the resting place of Spencer Goodman, the guy who looked like my childhood friend.

And over by the road lies Kenneth McDuff. The guy buried next door doesn't have a name, but pity his poor soul.

It troubled me that I could discover the crime of Tillman Simmons in a couple of seconds and not remember some of those men I saw executed. What does that say about me? Is it normal that I've forgotten? Maybe there's something wrong with me, or maybe it's to be expected, given that there were just so many. I tell people I saw 280 people executed, but the truth is I don't really know. It might be 278, it might be 283. But if you're a journalist, you don't remember everybody you've interviewed; if you're a surgeon, you don't remember everybody you've operated on.

They're all there, in a big, red filing cabinet in my office. But sometimes I'll pull out a file, read the notes in my own handwriting, all the accompanying documents, and still remember nothing about watching them die. When I got home from Peckerwood Hill that day, I opened up that filing cabinet, which is ready to burst, to get a few facts straight. In Napoleon's mugshot, he looks confounded, and repentant. But maybe that's just what I want to think, because Gary Graham's expression doesn't look too much different. In fact, you could define most of the mugshot expressions as 'doomed'. The day that picture was taken was the beginning of the end. It was the end, at least of any life worth living.

I discovered that the last inmate I saw die wasn't George Rivas, as I'd thought, but a guy named Keith Thurmond, who I had no recollection of whatsoever. It tells you how shattered I was, that the memories weren't even going in, never mind disappearing. Thurmond murdered his wife and her boyfriend in a fit of jealous rage, after they moved in together across the street. Despite all the evidence pointing towards him, he angrily protested his innocence on the gurney. According to my notes, the last words I heard in the death chamber were, 'Go ahead and finish it off… you can taste it.'

But where was the man whose name and crime I couldn't remember, but whose face was etched on my mind for all time? I could still see him, staring at the ceiling, a single tear running down his cheek. I could still visualise the witness room, containing nobody he knew. But he remained elusive. Maybe he deserved to be so lonely and forgotten. Or maybe it was my job to remember.

I began pulling files, eliminating the maddest, baddest and most notorious; the men who'd written me letters, intrigued me with their intellect, made me laugh. And then I found him: Caruthers 'Gus' Alexander, still young in his mugshot, but with the same unmistakable contours, and only second alphabetically in my cabinet. I could have saved myself a lot of searching.

In the early hours of 23 April 1981, Alexander collided with the car of a nightclub waitress named Lori Bruch. Prosecutors said he lured her from her vehicle, tied her up, raped and strangled her to death. Two children found Bruch's naked body in a flooded gutter the following morning. She had a two-year-old son. Alexander was on death row for 18 years before DNA testing proved him guilty. He called the results 'bunk'. According to his attorney, he was intelligent, articulate, good-natured, likeable and unlikely to reoffend. He was executed on 29 January 2001. A clipping from the *Item*, written by me, says the execution was witnessed by members of Bruch's family, and it troubles me greatly that I can't remember them being there. But I was right in that nobody was there for Alexander.

At the time of his arrest, Alexander had a common-law wife and two stepchildren, who would have been adults when he was put to death. I wonder if they forgot about him and moved on, or if he told them not to come. I wonder if I walked past his little stone, up on Peckerwood Hill, that nobody ever visits. I wonder if his execution made anything better. Did it give his victim's family peace? Did it make anyone feel victorious? Or was Napoleon Beazley right? Did it just make victims of all of us?

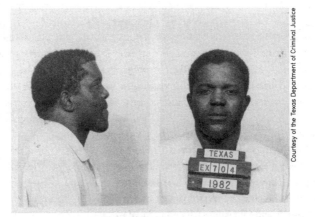

Caruthers 'Gus' Alexander's prison mugshots

ACKNOWLEDGEMENTS

When I first left my job at TDCJ, I was in a state of mourning – confused about what had happened to me, who I was and what would become of me. Compounding that state of grief was the bombardment of memories of all that I had seen, suddenly hitting me from all sides – and I didn't know exactly what to make of it. I only knew that I needed to try and put it in some order, so I could work through it and move on.

Cue my dear friend Pamela Colloff, then a reporter with the award-winning *Texas Monthly* magazine. While speaking with the extraordinarily talented Pam on another story for which she was gathering information, I mentioned to her all the thoughts I had been having about these executions I had seen – all the pictures and scenes that kept crossing my mind and how the same thing had been happening to Larry for years. When Pam suggested a story, I knew it might be my opportunity to get the tangled mess out of my head and into some shape that might make sense. We spent hours chatting, the result of which became the article 'The Witness', published in *Texas Monthly*'s September 2014 issue. I will be eternally grateful to Pam for putting our story to paper – it was such a cathartic experience just telling some of those stories out loud, both for Larry and myself, and I know I speak for both of us when I say that we love you dearly.

In February 2016, Ed Hancox directed and produced a beautiful segment on our dear Larry Fitzgerald for the BBC, called *The Man Who Witnessed 219 Executions*, which was viewed by Nick Walters, the man I now know and adore as my brilliant agent with David Luxton Associates. After watching this BBC documentary, Nick found our *Texas Monthly* article, and then he found me. He introduced himself and asked the magic question, 'Have you ever thought of writing a book?' And the rest is history. Thank you, Nick, for your vision, and for working so tirelessly on behalf of Larry and myself. You have been our advocate and, truly, this book would not have been were it not for you.

Thank you to the wonderful Kelly Ellis, editorial director, and the amazing Beth Eynon, editor, with Blink Publishing. You both have been so dedicated to this project and your enthusiasm has been infectious. I have always known we are in good hands and have trusted you every step of the way – thank you for making this possible and for taking such good care of us.

And then there's Benjamin Dirs, who had one of the trickiest tasks of all as my ghostwriter, in that you had to transcribe hours of interviews with me after realising that I speak twice as fast as any other American. Between copious amounts of laughter and alcohol, we managed to forge a bond I have no doubt will last a lifetime. From alligator farms to absinthe houses, tapas bars to beer gardens, voodoo shops to some of the shadiest bars one could ever set foot in, we have had some wonderful adventures. When you miss me, play some Glen Campbell and think of me, knowing that I'll beat your ass at Scrabble every single time. Thank you for all your work on this – I know you gave it your all.

To my mom and dad, who have always been the foundation upon which I have built my life. I kept putting off writing this because of you, because how do you find the words to thank the two people who gave you everything? Every time things have fallen apart, you have been there to put me back together. And every time things have worked out, I've always seen you right there, cheering me on. I love you both more than words can say, and I thank you more than I can ever express, for all you have given me, all you have taught me and for all of your love. Just know that everything I am is because of you... except the cursing – that's all me. I love you so very much.

To my brother, my best friend, who has always been DSD1 (if you don't know what that means it's okay, because it wasn't meant for you). You always know exactly when I need a kick in the ass to keep me going – you never let me feel sorry for myself for too long. And I always know there's no one more proud of me than you – I hope you know that it goes both ways. There's no one who makes me laugh like you, and no one who will ever know me like my little brother does. Love you, 'mano.

To my daughter, my heart, you are my reason for living and why I do everything I do. When you were little, you told me that you thought God had a cabinet full of little drawers and he pulled each child out and put them with the parents he thought they should have, and that's how he picked you for me – and I couldn't agree more. You were always meant to be mine, and I was always meant to be yours. I am so proud of you, and so proud to be your mother – there are no words to express my love for you. I love you.

To the rest of my family and dear friends, I have always believed we are shaped by those we love and who love us, and I have been very lucky to be surrounded by a wonderful and supportive family, and some of the greatest friends. Thank you all for loving and accepting me for all my quirks and flaws – for having my back and loving me even when I'm not my most lovable.

And lastly, to the men and women of the Texas Department of Criminal Justice, who do a mostly thankless job in the interest of public safety: thank you for your hard work and your sacrifice, protecting the people of the great state of Texas. You work long hours with little pay, you miss holidays with your families and you put your lives on the line to protect ours. Thank you for your service.